So Nuala
November ...

love Dad.

How Can We Create
a Just Society?

Other titles in the
Scripture for Living series

How Can We Create a Just Society?

Frank Turner SJ

DARTON, LONGMAN AND TODD
LONDON

First published in 1992 by
Darton, Longman and Todd Ltd
89 Lillie Road, London SW6 1UD

© 1992 Frank Turner sj

ISBN 0–232–51954–4

A catalogue record for this book is available
from the British Library

The Scripture quotations are taken from the
New Jerusalem Bible, published and copyright 1985 by
Darton, Longman and Todd Ltd and Doubleday & Co Inc
and used by permission of the publishers

Cover: *Empty Hands* by Sarah John

Thanks are due to the following for permission to quote
copyright material: HarperCollins Publishers from
An American Childhood by Annie Dillard; Michael Joseph Ltd from
A Book of Spells by Sara Maitland (1987); Sheed and Ward Ltd and
Penguin Books from *Pedagogy of the Oppressed* by Paulo Freire.

Phototypeset in 10/11½ pt Trump by Intype, London
Printed and bound in Great Britain
at the University Press, Cambridge

Contents

Introduction

◆━━▶

THE WRITINGS OF THE BIBLE – the Scriptures – are the Word of God. They are of supreme importance to all Christians and to all who wish to know and understand the meaning of Christianity. The Bible should be in every Christian home. Every aspect of Christian life and worship should reflect in some way what God says to his people. Catholics have not always been very good at reading and studying the Bible. In 1965 during the Second Vatican Council a document on Scripture as the Word of God (*Dei Verbum*) was published. This has had a marked effect in laying the foundations for an official programme of encouragement to Catholics to make the Bible central to their lives.

Much has happened since then. Every public act of worship has its reading from Scripture. Scripture (both Old and New Testaments) has a significant place in all religious education programmes, whether for adults or for children. The lectionary for the readings at daily and Sunday Mass covers a large amount of Scripture during its three-year cycle. Familiar acts of devotion like the Rosary and the Stations of the Cross have become far more scripturally based.

The positive value of this is obvious enough. But it has also meant that many Catholics have been thrown in at the deep end. They are a little like the Ethiopian in his carriage on the way home from Jerusalem who was reading some Scripture. Philip the Deacon heard him and asked him if he understood what he was reading. 'How can I', the man said, 'unless I have someone to guide me?' (Acts 8:26–40). Most of us do need help if we are to understand what we are reading. It is not that the language of Scripture is particularly difficult; it is rather that its context is so often unfamiliar.

I warmly welcome this series of *Scripture for Living*. Its particular value is that it helps us to see how Scripture is relevant to our daily lives. There are many other books for scholars. This series is for ordinary Christians who treasure Scripture, know for certain that it is of fundamental importance, but who are not sure how to make sense of what they read or how to relate it to their daily lives and experiences.

The pattern of the series is story, bible passage, commentary, reflection and prayer. There is a natural progression in this. The writings in the Bible (which form a whole library really) are about people trying to recognise God in their lives. So the context is just everyday life – the stuff of story. Story leads on naturally to Scripture because Scripture is itself about life in all its variety. So it speaks of love and hate, success and failure, death and resurrection; almost every imaginable human failing and strength finds place in it, simply because it is about real people. The commentary is an aid to understanding. Then, since the ultimate purpose of Scripture is to lead people closer to God, the text finishes with a prayer which ties together what has gone before and shows how our daily lives can be enriched.

The series is ideal for use in groups as well as by individuals. I wish it every success.

+ David Konstant
Bishop of Leeds

Preface

It MAY BE AS WELL to explain that this book does not pretend (or even intend) to offer a neat answer to the question posed in its title. That question will always be with us, and there is no full or final solution to be found – though I hope some of its aspects will be illuminated.

Instead, the title proposes one fundamental concern of Christian living, the attempt to create a just society, in view of which the Scriptures and our everyday experience will be examined. This perspective is indispensable. But every perspective is one among others, as is implied by this book's being one of a series. No single perspective can embrace the whole reality of our lives or the whole truth of Scripture.

The first two chapters are, in a sense, preliminary. The first, The Word of God, illustrates how Scripture and present-day personal experience can (and for Christians, must) be held together. The second, Work Force, offers a framework for interpreting that present-day experience, and, in doing so, it attempts to justify the book's particular focus on 'social justice'. Each subsequent chapter engages in a two-way process. Various aspects of injustice, justice, and the struggle for justice will be considered in the light of Scripture; but these experiences will in turn determine the standpoint from which we interpret Scripture.

We cannot live and make sense of our lives without the help of other people. Likewise, the Scriptures are a gift of God to *communities* of believers. In preparing this book I have been especially helped by several friends and colleagues in Manchester and Leeds. I hope they will recognise how much it owes to them. I am also grateful for the encouragement of Morag Reeve, my editor at Darton, Longman and Todd.

Many other people over the years will have contributed to this book unwittingly: but I must emphasise that the 'contemporary stories' are fictional and the characters in them invented. Where they are suggested by 'real life' events or conversations, the circumstances have been altered – to protect the innocent, as it were. For in order to make their point, stories so short have to oversimplify the issues involved and to disregard alternative, and possibly valid, ways of interpreting the situation. But then, the same goes for the gospel parables themselves.

FRANK TURNER SJ

The Word of God

As THE OLD SLUMS had been cleared, the inner-city area served by St Thomas's parish had become depopulated. Its remaining churchgoers were all older people, and an outsider might have thought that the parish had little future. But many of the surviving parishioners knew each other well, and the parish was important to them. Father Scott had been parish priest for about fifteen years, and was respected and popular. Long-standing groups such as the St Vincent de Paul Society still flourished, and there was a lively social life centred around frequent jumble sales.

The style of prayer and liturgy was traditional. You would often see people saying the rosary during Mass, rather than listening to the Scripture readings and homily (it was difficult to be surprised by Father Scott's sermons, of course, after fifteen years of them). There had, however, been some recent liturgical changes. Those attending daily Mass said Morning Prayer together using the psalms of the Office, and the Evening Prayer of the Church was said once a week during Benediction.

People in the parish were upset and angry about the City Council's plan to build a motorway right through the area. Much of the remaining housing would be demolished as a result, and the roadworks (and eventually the road itself) would split the parish in two. As always, no one seemed to have consulted local residents about this plan, so when the diocesan Justice and Peace Commission held its annual meeting in the city, it was natural to include the roadbuilding scheme on the agenda. Because of this item, a few parishioners of St Thomas's decided to attend.

In exploring the issue, the meeting first looked at the recent history of the local community itself, and how local people felt about the scheme. The group tried to collect all the information it could about the motorway scheme – its declared purpose, how long construction would take, what disruption to the neighbourhood would result, what jobs would be created (and who would get them), and so on. At this point, the group leader suggested giving some time to 'theological reflection': what light, for instance, might the Scriptures throw on the issue? During the discussion, some-one claimed that the local community could look at the issue in the light of the 'Magnificat', the prayer made by Mary in the gospel of Luke. Weren't the planners arrogant, paying no attention to the needs and views of the people who had most to lose? If so, couldn't you say that God was on the side of those who, it seemed, didn't count?

The group from St Thomas's was both intrigued and taken aback by this suggestion. 'I know we often say this prayer in church', said one, 'but I've never looked at it *this* way before. Surely, it's Our Lady's prayer, not ours, and she isn't the kind of person who stirs things up.'

'If you think about it, though', said another, 'she doesn't mince her words, does she? She's asking for a different kind of world than any *I* know!'

'No', someone else argued, 'she doesn't just *ask* for it, she thanks God that it's already arrived! Seems far-fetched to me.'

◆━━━━▶

And Mary said:

My soul proclaims
    the greatness of the Lord
and my spirit rejoices
    in God my Saviour;
because he has looked upon

the humiliation of his servant.
Yes, from now onwards
all generations will call me blessed,
for the Almighty
has done great things for me.
Holy is his name,
and his faithful love extends age after age
to those who fear him.
He has used the power of his arm,
he has routed the arrogant of heart.
He has pulled down princes
from their thrones
and raised high the lowly.
He has filled the starving with good things,
sent the rich away empty.
He has come to the help
of Israel his servant,
mindful of his faithful love
— according to the promise
he made to our ancestors —
of his mercy to Abraham
and to his descendants for ever.
(Luke 1:46–55)

The Christian Churches accept the Bible as the 'Word of God'. But it is a human document too, a confession of faith. It is also a complex work of literature, on which many human authors and editors have worked, most of them unknown to us. The English title 'The Bible' comes from the Greek *ta Biblia*, meaning simply 'The Books'. It contains prayers and hymns, stories (histories, but also legends and fictions), poems, meditations, passages of abstract argument, letters of encouragement or rebuke: there are even summarised legal codes, though these are not precise enough to determine the actual decisions of a court. Naturally, these different kinds of writing cannot all be interpreted in the same way. What we call 'Scripture', then, is made up of various components: it follows from this that we shall not easily be able to identify any single 'meaning of the Bible'; perhaps it even follows that such a single meaning cannot be stated at all.

Even if we could arrive at a reading of the Scriptures we all agreed on, our task would not be complete, for they demand much more from us than understanding alone. Ephesians 6:17 speaks of 'the sword of the Spirit, that is, the word of God', and according to Hebrews 4:12, 'The Word of God is something alive and active: it cuts more incisively than any two-edged sword'. These expressions suggest that we should not read Scripture just to be pleased by rich and stylish prose, or to be informed or moved, but we should read it *to be changed*. To put this point another way, 'the Word of God' does not simply lie there on the page. The Scriptural text *becomes* the Word of God (and it becomes the word *of God*) when, and only when, God is revealed to us through it. We never read or hear the Bible correctly without, so to speak, glimpsing in it the presence of God.

This claim itself leads to further difficulties. Firstly, how do we know that we perceive the true God through the text, and not some false god? The God who *seems* to be revealed in some Scriptural texts is one that many of us would have serious qualms about worshipping. For example he (definitely 'he'!) sometimes appears as a cruel war-god (see the words spoken to Saul in 1 Samuel 15:1–12), or as one who demands the inhuman treatment of women (as in the instructions given to Moses in Numbers 5:11–31). When we read such accounts of God and God's will, we might well want to object, with the character in *Porgy and Bess*, 'The things that yo' li'ble/To read in the Bible,/It ain't necessarily so'. Such a divinity differs utterly from that God who offers salvation to all people, who is 'infinitely loving', or 'full of mercy'. And yet we derive these more hopeful conceptions of God, like the others, from Scripture.

A second difficulty is connected with the first. Those listening to sermons in church do not have the right of reply, still less the right to heckle. For many of us, therefore, our formative experience of Scripture is of being *preached at*. We might be led to suppose that the Bible is a body of writing whose meaning is already settled by someone else, by 'the Church', perhaps (by which we may mean the clergy, or Church officials). This common conception cannot explain how *the Church itself* learns to interpret Scripture; it neglects the vital truth that if *we* are to be judged or changed by the Scriptures as individuals, the same goes for the whole Church, especially its teachers. Just as importantly, it overlooks the fact that those who never actively share in shaping the meaning of Scripture are psychologically unlikely to be able to take it seriously at all.

It is clear that much depends on who interprets the text and how. As it happens, the Scriptures themselves throw some light on the question of who understands them rightly. Our term 'gospel' renders a Greek word which literally means 'good news'. Now it seems that those people in the Bible who actually do regard revelation as 'good news' (rather than, say, as a condemnation or a warning of catastrophe) tend to be those in a certain kind of situation, and those with a certain kind of attitude. They have to be in some sense like 'little children', since, according to a key saying in Matthew 11:25, Jesus blesses the Father for 'hiding these things from the learned and the clever and revealing them to little children'. They have 'to look forward to deliverance'; that is, they have to know that they *need* the saving power of God, and have to long for this salvation. Thirdly, the Scriptures are interpreted rightly by those 'on whom the Spirit rests'; and this Spirit is described in 2 Corinthians 3:17 as the Spirit of freedom, through whom people receive either the gift of freedom itself or the courage to seek it.

Two attitudes are consistently contrasted in the Scripture. Take as an example the account, in the gospel of Luke, of the birth and infancy of Jesus. On one side, we have Elizabeth, Mary, Zechariah, Simeon and Anna. Elizabeth is filled with the Spirit and recognises the fruit of Mary's womb as the blessed one (*Luke* 1:41–2). Zechariah blesses God for 'setting free' the people according to the promise (1:68–70). Similarly, Simeon 'was a upright and devout man;

he looked forward to the restoration of Israel and the Holy Spirit rested on him'; and Anna praised God 'and spoke of the child to all who looked forward to the deliverance of Jerusalem' (2:25, 38). Opposed to these people is Herod, who when he learns of the birth of Jesus takes it as a grim threat. It draws from him not praise or rejoicing, but brutal action to *suppress* what is new. Far from 'looking forward to the deliverance of Jerusalem', he is bent only on staying in power. In the language of Mary's prayer, he is one of the rich who are to be 'sent away empty'.

Her prayer shows that Mary is one of those to whom the revelation is especially given. But, we must add, if it is given to her, it is also *hers to interpret*. The Spirit who has 'covered her with its shadow' (1:35) is 'the Spirit of freedom', and we find that she uses Scripture with great freedom. Her prayer assembles phrases drawn from several parts of the Hebrew Bible. (We realise from this that Mary knows the Scriptures intimately and is at home with them, that she treasures the 'Word of God' in her heart as she will later treasure the words of Jesus.) But she does not merely quote the prayers of others. She gives these phrases a *new* meaning, the meaning she now finds in her own life; and in turn she interprets the events of her life in the light of Jewish scriptural faith. In other words, she does not simply interpret the text of Scripture itself, but *interprets her own life in the light of Scripture*. In this way, she becomes a model for us: it is one way in which we can understand the traditional claim that she is 'mother of the Church'.

She draws especially on the prayer of Hannah (1 Samuel 2:1–10), which, in turn, is rooted in Hannah's own life. According to the biblical story, Hannah had been made barren by Yahweh, and was taunted for this by Peninnah, her servant. Hannah finally conceived a child, Samuel, when 'Yahweh remembered her'. She sees her deliverance from childlessness as a demonstration of how God truly acts in the world: God 'raises the poor from the dust', reverses the world's unjust order so decisively that:–

The full fed
   are hiring themselves out for bread
but the hungry need labour no more;
the barren woman bears sevenfold
but the mother of many is left desolate.
                       (1 Samuel 2:5)

Mary believes that God has 'looked down' on her, in the same way as God 'remembered' Hannah. And Mary is, indeed, portrayed as one who is exposed to danger and hardship by the actions of the arrogant, by distant political rulers whose power threatens the lives of countless others – and especially the lives of the poor.

The Roman Emperor, for instance, has decreed a census. The decision, so simple for him, means for Mary a harsh and dangerous journey through bandit country, close to her time of labour. The threat from Herod, of course, is still more terrible. He orders a mass murder in a ruthless attempt to avert any threat to his supremacy. This is the context in which we see Mary, the 'lowly one' who can militantly praise God for 'pulling down princes from their thrones': the phrase recalls the prayer of Hannah, but also shows Mary's awareness that God wills the *overthrow* of tyrants, not their protection. Her 'spirit rejoices' at the help, promised to 'our ancestors' and now actually given to Israel (in the birth of Jesus, whose very name means 'God saves'); she believes that God alone can save, and therefore that Israel cannot and need not look to the present rulers for the salvation that they would claim to guarantee.

To return to our story of St Thomas's: no matter how carefully we submit Mary's prayer to 'theological reflection', nothing in it will show us whether the road through the parish ought to be built or not, or what the local community ought to do about the matter. We can never expect Scripture to make our decisions for us, and can never straightforwardly read off from it clear instructions for our own actions or moral choices. The reasons for this derive from the nature of Scripture itself.

The Scriptures, including the sayings of Jesus himself, address people or communities in particular circumstances. But these circumstances are not ours; and the words of Scripture cannot in themselves indicate how they might best be interpreted in different situations and at other periods of history.

Also, if we *were* furnished with clear-cut divine commands or guidelines for action by the Bible, our own capacity for reason (which is itself God's gift) and our own freedom to seek and choose the good would be bypassed. We could then bring nothing creative to the decisions we have to make. In that case, 'revelation' would diminish our lives, not enrich them. It would be difficult to regard such 'revelation' as a gift of 'the Spirit of freedom'.

Finally, it is clear that the people of biblical times imagine God as one who acts directly in the world. For example, God is said to make some women barren and others fertile (or to make Hannah first barren and then fertile); today we should probably say that such things occur through 'natural causes', whether or not we can, in fact, understand those causes: again, Mary appeals to a God who 'pulls down princes from their thrones', whereas we would say that the overthrowing of rulers was something brought about by the action of *human persons*, individually or collectively. Despite this changed mentality, we can still properly have faith that 'God acts through us', because we believe that our own identity and acts can be grounded in God's very self: but few people now suppose that God is one separate cause of events among others. Whereas people in the Bible often seem to wait for God to act, we have *to act in the power of God*; which means, in turn, that we must recognise our own responsibility for the choice of such action.

If we accept these points about the nature of Scripture, they prompt an obvious series of questions. Just what *is* the point of reading the Scriptures? Why don't we simply go ahead and make the best decision we can, without expecting these ancient writings to help us? Is the 'theological reflection' recommended to the group from St Thomas's just a waste of time?

If we do continue to look to the Scriptures, it is because we take them to offer a special insight, a 'revelation', into the nature of God's self and God's will; and also, therefore, into the very foundations of our own lives. If this is the case, Scripture can enlighten us, encourage and strengthen us, challenge us. In this book we shall be exploring some examples of how this might happen. Meanwhile, to illustrate the potential power of Scripture, we return to Mary's prayer, to ask what light it might cast on the problem of urban roadbuilding!

Building an urban motorway is not just a matter of surveying and engineering. The project needs to be seen at many levels. The road would never be built, for instance, unless someone with influence expected to gain from it. Supposing that some people support and others oppose its being built, who decides, and how? What are some alternative uses of the many millions of pounds which must be spent on it? Someone might reply that questions like these are 'political' and are therefore none of our business – or, at least, none of the Church's business. We will look at that point of view more carefully in the next chapter. At this point it is sufficient to say that to take this position would mean treating certain institutions ('the Council', say, or 'the Government') as beyond challenge. But since institutions like these are elected by, and claim to act in the name of, the people, they must therefore be held to be accountable to those people.

In reality, the freedom of action of 'those in power' is quite limited, since they have to respond to those who can make their demands count. A former President of the USA, Franklin D. Roosevelt, is said to have told a group of lobbyists, 'O.K., you've persuaded me. Now go out and put pressure on me.' On the whole the middle classes, and 'important' people such as the directors of large companies, know that they can exercise a significant degree of control over political decisions. But the poor can be quite slow to learn this. Proclaiming 'the greatness of the Lord' might teach us to mistrust the claims of *other* would-be lords. We shall then be less inclined to identify the decisions of the powerful with 'the will of God'. Nor will we falsely suppose that the ideal of 'humility' requires us to surrender all control over our personal and communal lives to 'the arrogant of heart' who are all too ready to claim it. In this way, Scripture can transform our 'hearts', that is our attitudes, our entire way of thinking and acting. Such a transformation would, not least, affect the way in which the local community entered the process of deciding how (or whether) the road might be built.

FOR REFLECTION

1. To what extent are you aware that the Scriptures are relevant to those matters which most deeply concern you at present?
2. When you have heard homilies based on the Scriptures, is it often your experience that you are helped to reflect for yourself on the Scripture? Or do you feel you are 'told what to think'?
3. Do you see the Bible as a book which provides you with reliable rules of conduct? If so, which parts of it influence you most?

PRAYER

Send your Spirit on us, Lord, so that we may be filled with your truth and love. Through our reading and hearing of the Scripture, may we learn to be aware that you are present and active in us, sustaining us in our joys and our struggles. We make this prayer through your son Jesus, himself the Word of God, who became flesh and lived among us.

Work Force

RAYMOND WAS A middle manager in an electronics company, where there had been a serious industrial dispute. It was less about actual pay levels than about pay structures. The management had proposed to reduce basic pay as a proportion of total pay, and to increase the piece-work element. The proposal came without warning and was presented as non-negotiable, as an essential means of remaining competitive in an international market. The unions wanted to retain the existing pay structure: a substantial basic wage, with the option of overtime and possible productivity bonuses. Eventually the union had ordered a work-to-rule, and the company had responded by imposing a lock-out. As a company director had said to Raymond, 'We have to show these upstarts that management has the right to manage'.

Thinking this over, Raymond recalled his business trip to South Korea the year before. He had been shown round a plant similar to his own. There was no accredited trades union, no paid sick leave, no pension plan. The shop-floor workers were almost all women in their teens and twenties. Raymond was told that assembling microchips so strained the eyes that most people's sight was too poor to do the work by the time they were thirty or so. It was easy enough to fire them at that point, said his guide reassuringly, since there was never a shortage of teenagers who needed jobs.

Raymond began to realise that his firm would like to have been able to import the South Korean system into Britain.

The thought disturbed him, but what could a middle manager do about it? His job was to implement policy, not make
it. In a way, he was in the same position as the Korean
women: if he couldn't do his job, plenty of others would be
keen to replace him.

◄————►

*Then there came to power in Egypt a new king who had
never heard of Joseph. 'Look,' he said to his people, 'the
Israelites are now more numerous and stronger than we
are. We must take precautions to stop them from increasing
any further, or if war should break out, they might join the
ranks of our enemies. They might take arms against us and
then escape from the country.'*

*Accordingly they put taskmasters over the Israelites to
wear them down by forced labour. In this way they built
the store-cities of Pithom and Rameses for Pharaoh. But
the harder their lives were made, the more they increased
and spread, until people came to fear the Israelites. So the
Egyptians gave them no mercy in the demands they made,
making their lives miserable with hard labour: with dig-
ging clay, making bricks, doing various kinds of field-work
– all sorts of labour that they imposed on them without
mercy.*

(Exodus 1:8–14)

◄————►

When Jesus was asked what one must do to inherit eternal
life, he turned the question back on the enquirer, who
answered correctly, 'You must love the Lord your God with
all your heart, with all your soul, with all your strength,
and with all your mind, and your neighbour as yourself'
(Luke 10:27). The parable of the 'good Samaritan' which
follows answers the question '*Who* is my neighbour?', and
teaches that a 'neighbour' is not simply one who happens
to live nearby or to belong to one's own circle, but is anyone
who acts as neighbour to us, and also anyone for whom we
are willing to act as neighbour. In other words, we must

not set limits in advance to the categories of people we are to 'love'. This claim, in turn, implies that the word 'love' must have a more extended application than we are accustomed to give it. So there arises a second question: '*How are we to love our neighbour?*'. It seems, in reply to this, that we cannot rule out any course of action which genuinely tends to their well-being.

What, then, is 'well-being'? Each of our lives, and therefore the true good of each of us, has several dimensions. The following analysis of those dimensions underlies much of this book. The various strands may usefully be distinguished from each other, but they must never be split apart:

i) *Our bodily life.* We are not 'persons who own bodies', as if our bodies were somehow detached from our personal identities. Our experience is *embodied* experience, our perceptions and thoughts are inseparable from our senses, from their openness to the world and their active response to it. 'The good' in this dimension of our lives is of at least two kinds: firstly, the fulfilment of such basic bodily needs as food and drink, shelter, warmth and clothing, fresh air and clean water; secondly, the freedom from violence, imprisonment, serious illness or disability (or, put positively, the gift of appropriate vigour for our time of life), and so on. A certain carelessness of our own real needs may sometimes be admirable, if it stems from our free striving for some greater good, or it may be wrongful, if it merely expresses a lack of respect for ourselves. The neglect of *others'* basic needs is almost always evil.

ii) *Our interior 'spiritual' state.* We are not human apart from our unique 'inner life': our consciousness, our joys and sorrows, our dreams, our hopes and fears. 'The good' here will include such elements as freedom from disabling fear, from despair, from the terrible sense that life is futile or meaningless.

iii) *Our personal relationships.* It is false to think of ourselves as essentially isolated persons who just happen to meet others. On the contrary, we are simply not fully human, we have no 'human life', apart from our particular relationships with other people. These relationships may be casual (with shop assistants, or with people we 'know' only on the telephone), or intimate (with our spouse or children). In either case, they are part of *who we are*. In this realm of personal relationships, 'the good' means such qualities as courtesy and respect, a capacity for warmth, tenderness and loyalty, a freedom from bitterness, from overdependence on others, from the desire to dominate them or manipulate them for our own purposes.

iv) *Our lives as members of society.* The society in which we live is not merely a stage or backdrop, against which we live out our independent lives as individuals. Our society affects our lives at their very heart, and it is we, together, who are 'society'. In Hitler's Germany, people's 'Jewish' or 'Aryan' identity must have determined many of their most private experiences: just as, according to the first chapter of Exodus, it made a profound difference whether one was born an Israelite or an Egyptian. In other words, we are related to other people as *members of groups* which affect each others' lives for better or worse. It follows that we are truly involved with, and related to, people we shall never meet face to face. In this dimension of our lives, 'the good' may be conceived in terms of 'justice': for example, as deliverance from exploiting others (systematically benefiting from their suffering) or being exploited by them.

v) *Our life as dwellers on earth.* Once again, the fact that we inhabit the earth is not incidental to our lives, but is of their essence. We rely on the earth to support us, and we cannot survive if we destroy it. We are the children and tenants of the earth rather than its owners. Even the specific good of the human species, therefore, requires freedom from the greed that ruins or pollutes our own habitat. We need to cultivate both respect for the earth and appreciation of its beauty.

It is obvious that the fifth category overlaps with the fourth. Pollution, in the end, always harms other people, often the poor who have no means to escape it. But in fact all the categories constantly overlap, because our lives are a unity which we lead in all five dimensions at once. A person's 'sexual life', for instance, has obvious bodily and inter-personal aspects. But our sexuality is lived out also in our inmost 'psyche', in our daydreams and our fears. It is equally lived out in our membership of society, for our gender conditions many of the roles we inhabit, and the patterns of behaviour expected of us. We might react by conforming to these expectations, or challenging them, but we cannot help being affected by them.

It is possible for our horizons to shrink, so that we neglect life in one or more dimensions. This is natural for brief periods – it's all right if falling in love temporarily distracts us from local politics! – but is damaging if it persists. We recognise the narrowness of the 'food freak', the hypochondriac, the ruthless executive with no time for his family.

Returning to our main argument, we tend to use the word 'love' to refer specifically to the third category, to apply only to our most important and intimate personal relationships. But the 'love' commanded in Luke 10 is the Greek *agape*, which refers to the whole of our conduct towards other people. We love them by willing their good and striving for it, in innumerable ways. 'Social justice', in the light of the gospel, is in the first place simply that form of love which is due between *groups of people*. Therefore we can say that the struggle for social justice is something to which our faith commits us. This book focuses on this struggle, this particular dimension of Christian faith and love, without at all denying the other dimensions discussed above.

It is clear that the forces of justice and injustice are present in our everyday, secular world, wherever people are healed and cherished, or damaged and victimised. The action of God which liberates Israel from Egypt puts right a situation in which the Israelites were enslaved in both a religious and a practical, 'secular' way. According to Exodus

5:1–5 and 1:15–22, they were forbade the worship of God which was precious to them. They were also physically oppressed, even as far as being threatened with genocide. Today, also, Christian faith must find expression in the secular world, as well as in directly 'religious' activity, for God's Spirit is at work far beyond the special sphere of the Churches, as well as within it. For this reason, the Second Vatican Council urged Christians to examine 'the signs of the times' in order to learn what the gospel asks of them.

It is natural for us to think that slavery is a thing of the past, that it cannot *today* be a 'sign of the times'. This is not wholly true. The *Shorter Oxford Dictionary* defines a slave in this way: 'One who is the property of, and entirely subject to, another person, whether by capture, purchase, or birth; a servant completely divested of freedom and personal rights'. Many people throughout the world fall in part within the scope of this definition, at least in their lives as employees. The South Korean women whose condition so touched Raymond *are* virtually divested of their freedom and their personal rights while at work, and their economic status and the lack of alternative employment available to them probably deprive them of effective freedom *from* work. They are therefore imprisoned in a specific employment situation in which they are without rights.

The situation of most black South African miners comes even closer to that of slavery, for they are often shackled far beyond the pit-head. Often, for instance, they have to tolerate long-term separation from their families, and the recent creation of 'homelands' within South Africa has deprived many of them of South African citizenship.

We cannot say that conditions like these are limited to the 'Third World'. In such countries as Switzerland and Germany, 'guest-workers' tend to get only the kind of jobs no one else will do, and may be sent home as soon as they lose their job through sickness or recession. Californian agriculture relies heavily on those who are termed 'undocumented aliens', or, in British usage, 'illegal immigrants'. Typically these 'aliens' are refugees from war or poverty in

Central and South America. For a while, the authorities may turn a blind eye to their presence in the USA. But they can expect deportation the day they fall ill or join a union. In Britain, too, many workers suffer from restricted employment rights. Many part-time employees (and almost all home-workers in industries such as clothing) have no holiday entitlement, no right to sick pay or maternity leave, and certainly no redundancy payments.

The harsh effects of industrial economies can persist despite dramatic political changes. Recently, the whole of Germany was elated as the Berlin Wall was smashed and the borders opened. But the new freedom of movement means that the most vulnerable workers in the former West Germany are being undercut by workers from the East, who will accept lower pay and worse conditions of employment. In turn, jobs in what was East Germany are sought by still poorer immigrants from Poland (who could be seen as equivalent to the South Korean teenagers of our story). It is right to acclaim the achievement of unification, but even genuine political improvements can be undermined or outweighed by the continued realities of economic power. So it turns out that the new 'freedom' brings immediate and tangible benefits *only to the affluent* – for example, to those German companies who can expand into the East, or to German shoppers who can now buy up Polish consumer goods at bargain prices.

What tends strongly to injustice is the concentration of power into a few hands. The Egyptians, claiming to fear the Israelites in the future, make brutal use of their own *present* power. In our story the argument to 'let management manage' pretends to be a harmless, commonsense plea for freedom to do a specialist job. But Raymond recognised that it expressed a disguised bid for absolute control of the company, as if such matters as pay, work rosters and conditions of employment were the management's business and no one else's.

The last twenty years, in Britain, have seen a prolonged onslaught on the trades unions. Phrases such as 'union barons' have become clichés. People have argued that powerful unions threaten the interests not only of industry, but of the workers themselves. It is quite possible for unions to damage the cause of workers: by discriminating against women, for instance, or by defending the differentials enjoyed by the best-paid. But it is idle to suppose that workers as a whole would be well served by the dismantling of the unions, which would leave management's power effectively unchecked. Contrary to what Raymond's boss might claim, managerial power is not simply innocent, or benevolent, or even neutral. It is, not least, *power over workers*. The 'Pharaoh' model of management inevitably brings enslavement with it.

One thing our story emphasises is that the struggle for social justice is not merely a Church struggle. It is being constantly waged around us, in society as a whole. For Christians, nevertheless, the struggle remains *a requirement of faith*. The Holy Spirit can be active, the life of God's Kingdom made present, not only in the projects of the churches, but also in such bodies as unions (and, for that matter, employers). Naturally, it may be difficult to see in any given case what we ought to support and what to oppose: but that is equally so in the internal affairs of the Church.

On the matter of industrialism itself, some forceful remarks are made in Pope John Paul II's letter of 1981, *On Human Work* (in Latin, *Laborem Exercens*). Workers, argues the Pope, were long regarded as an 'instruments of production', entirely at the disposal of their employers. This is a degraded conception, because the true *purpose* of all work is the human good, which does not exclude the worker's good. In addition, the worker is always the *subject* of work, not just its 'instrument'. The degraded view caused an 'unheard-of accompanying exploitation in the field of wages, working conditions and social security for the worker', which 'gave rise to a just social reaction and caused the impetuous emergence of a great burst of solidarity between workers'. Certainly there have been profound changes since the nineteenth century (brought about, not least, by the unions themselves). But various power systems 'have allowed flagrant injustices to persist or have created new ones'. Today also, 'there is a need for ever new movements of solidarity of the workers and with the workers'. The primary principle, according to *Laborem Exercens*, is 'the priority of labour over capital'.

Raymond's boss would be distinctly uneasy!

FOR REFLECTION

1. Do you instinctively think of religion as especially concerned with one or more of the 'five dimensions' but irrelevant to others? Do you think Christians often restrict the relevance of their faith in this way?
2. What could it mean to practise *agape* towards homeless or unemployed people? To your own employer/ employees? To the poor of a Third World country?
3. Consider how industrial disputes are usually reported, especially in the popular press. What conception of the nature of industrial work, and of the respective rights of managers and unions, is implied by the reports?

PRAYER

We recognise you, Lord God, as Lord of the whole of our lives, since they are entirely your gift. Help us to become increasingly aware of your presence and your saving action in all persons and things, so that we learn to do your will more fully.

The Chosen and Their Sins

AN ANIMAL RIGHTS GROUP launched a protest against a butcher's shop in the small shopping centre of a run-down council estate. The shopkeeper arrived one morning to find the words 'Blood on their Hands' painted in red on the shutter. A couple of days later, 'Scum' was added; and after a few more days, the slogan 'Family Butchers – Family Death Squads'. It is upsetting to be hated, and by this time the shop assistants were a little nervous. Was anyone watching them leave work? Might the next demonstration be directed at their own homes? The customers were sympathetic but also uneasy, since they too felt included in the accusations. The next week, the steel shutter was wrenched off and the shop smashed up.

It had already been difficult for the shop to get insurance cover. Now the insurance company told the butcher that their premiums would be doubled. As the company pointed out, it was obvious that the attackers intended to carry on until the shop was forced to close.

The staff met to decide what to do. They all wanted to hang on. None of them had any other trade. The shop-owner lived just a few streets away, and was proud of knowing most of his customers personally. But takings had been low even before the attacks, and the shop was struggling to survive. The customers were mainly the kind of local people who found it hard to get to the supermarket a mile away. They didn't own cars, and many of them were elderly; most didn't buy more than a few sausages, an occasional chop or a piece of chicken.

The shop struggled on for a while and then closed. Now there was no butcher within a mile or so, and the animal liberation group threw a party to celebrate. The shop-owner managed to get a job in the branch of a nationwide chain of butcher's shops in the city centre, but the two part-time assistants were unable to find work. It was the older local residents who really missed the shop. A few months later the newsagent also had to close down, when, because of the attacks, its insurance premiums were raised by fifty per cent, much more than the business could stand.

◆━━━◆

Abram's wife Sarai had borne him no child, but she had an Egyptian slave-girl called Hagar. So Sarai said to Abram, 'Listen, now! Since Yahweh has kept me from having children, go to my slave-girl. Perhaps I shall get children through her.' And Abram took Sarai's advice.

Thus, after Abram had lived in the land of Canaan for ten years, Sarai took Hagar her Egyptian slave-girl and gave her to Abram as his wife. He went to Hagar and she conceived. And once she knew she had conceived her mistress counted for nothing in her eyes. Then Sarai said to Abram, 'This outrage done to me is your fault! It was I who put my slave-girl into your arms but, now she knows that she has conceived, I count for nothing in her eyes. Yahweh judge between me and you!' 'Very well,' Abram said to Sarai, 'your slave-girl is at your disposal. Treat her as you think fit.' Sarai accordingly treated her so badly that she ran away from her . . .

Hagar bore Abram a son, and Abram gave his son borne by Hagar the name Ishmael. Abram was eighty-six years old when Hagar bore him Ishmael . . .

God spoke to him [Abram] as follows, 'For my part, this is my covenant with you: you will become the father of many nations. And you are no longer to be called Abram;

your name is to be Abraham, for I am making you father
of many nations . . .

Furthermore God said to Abraham, 'As regards your wife
Sarai, you must not call her Sarai, but Sarah. I shall bless
her and moreover give you a son by her. I shall bless her
and she will become nations: kings of peoples will issue
from her.' Abraham bowed to the ground, and he laughed,
thinking to himself, 'Is a child to be born to a man one
hundred years old, and will Sarah have a child at the age
of ninety?' . . .

Yahweh treated Sarah as he had said, and did what he
had promised her. Sarah conceived and bore Abraham a
son in his old age, at the time God had promised. Abraham
named the son born to him Isaac, the son to whom Sarah
had given birth . . .

The child grew and was weaned, and Abraham gave a
great banquet on the day Isaac was weaned. Now Sarah
watched the son that Hagar the Egyptian had borne to
Abraham, playing with her son Isaac. 'Drive away that
slave-girl and her son,' she said to Abraham, 'this slave-
girl's son is not to share the inheritance with my son Isaac.'
This greatly distressed Abraham, because the slave-girl's
child too was his son, but God said to him, 'Do not distress
yourself on account of the boy and your slave-girl. Do whatever Sarah says, for Isaac is the one through whom your
name will be carried on. But the slave-girl's son I shall also
make into a great nation, for he too is your child.' Early
next morning, Abraham took some bread and a skin of
water, and, giving them to Hagar, put the child on her
shoulder and sent her away.

She wandered off into the desert of Beersheba. When the
skin of water was finished she abandoned the child under
a bush. Then she went and sat down at a distance, about
a bowshot away, thinking, 'I cannot bear to see the child
die.' Sitting at a distance she began to sob.

(Genesis 16:1–6, 15–16; 17:3–5, 15–17; 21:1–3, 8–17)

⬦━━━⬦

These extracts come from the story of Abram, who becomes Abraham. The Abraham story winds through fifteen chapters of Genesis, interspersed with other material. The story's clearest theme is God's choice of Abraham as the one through whom the destiny of the Israelite people is brought about. The changes by which Abram becomes Abraham and Sarai becomes Sarah symbolise how their very identity is transformed, along with their role in the divine plan for Israel. So, Abram must leave his own country, for 'a country which I shall show you'. He is to renounce his security, risk the unknown, endure an exile's grim struggle for survival. But this divine commission is accompanied by a blessing: 'I shall make you a great nation, I shall bless you and make your name famous; you are to be a blessing!' When Abram reaches Canaan, God again assures him, 'I shall give this country to your progeny' (12:1–2, 7–8). From this viewpoint, the story concerns Abram's faith in the divine promise and the tests to which this faith is subjected.

So, for instance, famine drives him to abandon his country and flee to Egypt (12:10–20). Egypt is for him, as it will be later for the whole Israelite people, the place of testing. An element of suspense enters the story since, as we well know today, refugees rarely return home to prosperity. In fact, Abram has to act with ingenuity to avert the threat to his life (and therefore to his descendants, and to the promise itself). The later incident in which Sarah is promised a child when she is well past child-bearing age, like other such stories in the Bible, suggests that the child concerned is, in a more than ordinary sense, a gift of God. (Interestingly, it seems that both Abraham and Sarah 'fail' this trial of faith, as their bitter laughter indicates (17:17–18; 18:10–15). Finally, the famous story in chapter 22 demands from Abraham a level of faith which defies all odds: he must be willing to give up the life of his son Isaac in the belief that 'God will provide' descendants who may become a great nation. When Abraham's story is read in this way, he is seen as the triumphant if flawed hero of a kind of divine thriller: in fact, this is the interpretation adopted by an important passage of the New Testament, Hebrews 11:8–19.

Suppose, though, that we adopt Hagar's viewpoint. Everything suddenly changes. Abraham now appears more like an oppressor, a villain, than a 'hero of faith'. Sarai and Abram act as if they assume that God's promise to them permits them to treat Hagar as no more than a means to their goal; in effect, as a non-person. She can be sexually exploited for breeding purposes, then casually cast aside – and no one feels much remorse. Abram is both callous and cowardly (an ugly combination of qualities), ducking out of a marital row with the offhand pronouncement, 'Your slave-girl is at your disposal. Use her as you think fit'.

Later, Isaac is born by the special providence of God. Now, a divine gift, or 'grace', never becomes simply our own property. It is always given us to be shared generously with others. But Abraham and Sarah go to cruel lengths to *prevent* Hagar and Ishmael from sharing in the divine promise.

What is disturbing about the story is that it seems to disguise this cruelty, and to absolve the reader from judging it with clarity. Still worse, even *God* appears to collude in the victimising of Hagar. God's assurance to Abraham ('Do not distress yourself on account of the boy and the slave-girl') seems almost repulsive in the way that it values Abraham's peace of mind above Hagar's agony. However, the story does not give us direct access to the 'character' of God, only to the manner in which the writer (presumably one of the beneficiaries of 'the promise') *imagined* God; and as we have already seen we cannot regard all biblical representations of God as equivalently truthful.

Once we begin to look at Abraham less sympathetically, other strands of the Genesis narrative shift into prominence. Early on, while still in Egypt (in a story that is unfortunately omitted from the Lectionary of Mass Readings), Abram tries to protect himself by passing off Sarai as his sister, virtually offering her to Pharaoh. There is an ugly word for this kind of conduct (certainly not 'ingenuity', the word I used above when thinking of Abram as hero), and we might guess that Abram's slave is unlikely to be better treated than his wife. This earlier incident also helps to account for (if not excuse) Sarah's own blameworthy behaviour towards Hagar. Sarah is herself at grave risk, and it is not surprising when victims lash out to defend themselves. As a passage from *Tryptich*, a short story by Sara Maitland, sums up:

> Here we see, perhaps for the first time in recorded history, one of the classic devices used by men against women. Sarah, the wife, gets blamed but not punished. Hagar, the mistress, gets punished but not blamed. Abraham gets neither; he has his cake and eats it too. This is neat.

When we commit ourselves to social justice, we always need to take the 'perspective of Hagar'; of the one who is excluded, despised, disregarded. It is not the only valid perspective, but it is an essential one which we can easily overlook. A cause may be admirable without justifying all that is done in its name. In fact, idealists can be dangerously inclined to feel themselves exempt from ordinary concern for the rights of their opponents, or even their allies and co-workers. It can happen, for instance, that charitable or Church bodies pay their employees badly, or neglect to give them proper contracts of employment – as if anything were fair in pursuit of the Kingdom!

The Scriptures themselves offer a quite different model. The first 'Servant Song' (Isaiah 42:1–7) presents to us a mysterious figure who will bring justice to 'the nations', 'will not be crushed until he has established fair judgement on earth', yet 'does not break the crushed reed or snuff the faltering wick'. The Christian Church from its earliest days took this figure to be a symbol of Christ himself. As followers of Christ, we need to allow this image to challenge *ourselves*. How can we be courageous and effective workers for justice without becoming ruthless? How can we be compassionate without giving up the struggle?

In considering our story, we may assume that the cause of animal rights is a just and urgent one. There are serious moral questions to be asked of the huge international meat industry. Challenge, even direct confrontation, might well be called for. If we are serious about the issue, we shall also be willing to reconsider our own assumptions about the proper treatment of animals, about our own dietary needs, and so on. Neither of these approaches would offer easy answers; and both would demand our energy, intelligence and patience. It is much easier, but it is also gutless and futile, to launch a bitter and violent attack on the industry's weakest available representative. The animal rights group in our story is not (as it probably imagines) pluckily confronting the strongholds of power. It is *itself* acting as an oppressor and creating new victims.

What seems most destructive of all, perhaps, is that they call their opponents 'scum', as if they were assured of their own righteousness. The lie which attributes all guilt to others while assuming oneself to be pure, underpins many injustices. Certainly we (as individuals, as groups, as the Church) must not shy away from confronting the pressing political and economic issues of our time. But if we fight injustice with ruthlessness or hatred, and if we are blind to the people our own actions damage, we will not overcome injustice but merely displace or reinforce it.

FOR REFLECTION

1. Can you think of other people besides Hagar who seem to be treated unfairly by the writers of the Bible? Why might this happen?
2. Does a good end justify any efficient means of attaining it? How far can we be expected to take into account the personal needs and fears of our opponents?

PRAYER

We know, Lord, that we are sinners. Even when we search for justice we can be blind to the people we harm. Help us to learn from the prophet Micah the 'one thing' that you ask of us: to act justly, to love tenderly, and to walk humbly with our God.

Privilege and Prejudice

◆━━◆

THE DOORBELL RANG. It was Susan, a neighbour of Jane's, and she held up a petition she wanted signing. 'Sorry I haven't time to come in, I've a lot more calls to make. You know that big detached house at the corner of the street that's been up for sale for a couple of months? A voluntary group wants to buy it and convert it into a hostel. They want to put mental cases there, the ones who've been discharged from hospital. We've been told they've nearly raised enough money. Will you sign this petition? It's to make the Council refuse planning permission. We've already got forty names from round here.'

Jane didn't enjoy arguments, but she was uneasy. She thought for a moment. 'I may be wrong', she said, 'but didn't you canvass for the Council in the local elections last year?'

'That's right', Susan replied. 'I always seem to get involved in those kind of things – I think you have to do your bit for what you believe in.'

'But the Council were in favour of a community care policy, weren't they?' Jane asked.

Susan flushed. 'Yes, I see what you're getting at. But if that house is converted it could take anything up to a dozen people. This street is quiet and residential. It's not the best place for people like that to live.'

'But it won't be a *hospital*, will it?' said Jane. 'They'll just be residents, surely?'

'Fine', said Susan. 'I can see you don't want to sign, but

there's no need to preach about it.' She walked away and slammed the gate behind her.

◄═══►

Now it happened that on the way to Jerusalem he [Jesus] was travelling in the borderlands of Samaria and Galilee. As he entered one of the villages, ten men suffering from a virulent skin-disease came to meet him. They stood some way off and called to him, 'Jesus! Master! Take pity on us.' When he saw them he said, 'Go and show yourselves to the priests.' Now as they were going away they were cleansed. Finding himself cured, one of them turned back praising God at the top of his voice and threw himself prostrate at the feet of Jesus and thanked him. The man was a Samaritan. This led Jesus to say, 'Were not all ten made clean? The other nine, where are they? It seems that no one has come back to give praise to God, except this foreigner.' And he said to the man, 'Stand up and go on your way. Your faith has saved you'.

(Luke 17:11–19)

◄═══►

In the first chapter of this book, it was suggested that many Scripture passages come to us with a particular 'traditional' interpretation already built into them. This is not surprising, since the Christian Churches have read the Bible for two thousand years, regarding it as precious and never ceasing to reflect on it. These interpretations, however, can sometimes prevent us from fully experiencing the text for ourselves.

The familiar story of the ten men with skin disease (in other translations they are 'ten lepers') has usually been explained in some such way as this: 'Jesus healed ten people. But only one had the common decency to come back and thank him. Ingratitude is one of the most unattractive sins of all, and one of the most widespread. Think of all that God gives us, and then think how careless we sometimes are about prayer, about giving thanks. Even when we do pray it's usually just to ask for things. And think how easy it is, also, to take for granted other people and what they do for us.'

This explanation, obviously, is not 'wrong'. It is quite acceptable as far as it goes, and we may well need reminding of it. But what such an explanation does is to go straight for the 'moral' of the story, as if Scripture were only a set of veiled commandments which need to be uncovered, a moral code that needs cracking. This method of interpreting the Bible is tempting, because all of us would occasionally appreciate a neat and accessible 'key' to our moral dilemmas. The more guidelines the better, we might even imagine, so that the number of our uncertainties will be reduced. There is a good joke told about Moses coming down from Sinai: he shows the engraved Tablets of the Law to a priest, who pleads 'Isn't there room for just one more?'.

But if we moralise too quickly, we will miss much of what is most interesting about Scripture, and much of what it has to convey to us. Scripture is a revelation of *what life is like*. Much secular literature, similarly, aims to reveal truths about our lives. The Scriptures are special because they express that distinctive truth which is disclosed by the community's faith in God (and, in the case of the New Testament, the Christian community's faith in Jesus Christ). This truth concerns both the life of the everyday world, and the fulness of life which God intends for us. What is revealed, then, is the scope and richness of the entirety of our actual and potential lives, in so far as our lives are seen as a gift of God. The moral obligations which this gift of life imposes on us are genuine, but secondary.

A second and equally common way to narrow the application of Scripture is automatically to interpret it in individual terms. Take, for instance, a famous poetic passage of the book of Isaiah:

> Do not be afraid, for I have redeemed you;
> I have called you by your name,
>   you are mine.

> Should you pass through the waters,
>   I shall be with you;
> or through rivers,
>   they will not swallow you up.
>
>   (Isaiah 43:1–2)

This passage is often discussed as if it were addressed to certain private individuals: to those in trouble, for example, or to those beginning a retreat. Certainly it is true and important that God does 'call each of us by name'. According to John 10:3, for example, the true shepherd calls his sheep 'one by one' and leads them out. But in the passage from Isaiah the promise is actually made to the people, to Israel. Interestingly, those who read the Bible as a quarry of moral lessons also tend to treat it in this individualised manner, perhaps because moral appeals to large groups of people tend to strike us as hollow or absurd.

If we move beyond moralism and individualism, we can see that our passage from Luke is a story which reveals unpleasant truths about group behaviour, and also about ourselves as individuals who are liable to be dominated, perhaps unthinkingly, by our allegiance to certain groups. In Jesus' day those with skin diseases were regarded as ritually unclean and banned from the Temple. They were even banned from the cities, presumably because in a crowd it was difficult for the pious to identify them readily and keep their distance. Even in the countryside, as Luke makes clear, the sick men had to stand some way off and call out to Jesus.

Now, as we are told in John 4:9, Jews and Samaritans did not mix. But in Luke's story this taboo counts for nothing in the face of the more fundamental exclusion which the diseased men experience *in common*. As long as all of them are unclean, it is possible for the Samaritan to accompany the Jews. As all are marginalised, all can stay together. They can ask Jesus, 'Take pity on *us*'.

Then the ten are healed. The nine Jews are now able to take their place in the mainstream of Jewish religious life;

but the Samaritan is still excluded. Their separation from him becomes a religious duty, the necessary means of preserving their newly acquired ritual purity. The purpose of this separation, as we have seen, was to maintain the worship of God in its purity. But in the story it is self-defeating, preventing the true worship of God which religion is meant to nurture. 'No one has come back to give praise to God except this stranger', says Jesus. So, once before in the Bible, the Syrian, Naaman, returned to the prophet Elisha who had healed him, and said 'Now I know that there is no God anywhere on earth except in Israel' (2 Kings 5:15). Like Naaman, the Samaritan is not only healed, but comes to faith and is saved. For the nine Jews, on the contrary, healing, which is truly a sign of salvation, becomes a mere substitute for it. For they now falsely assume that they must seek salvation by maintaining their separation and their privilege.

We can often consign people to a race, a class, an income bracket, even a gender – 'You just can't argue with women, they get so emotional' – and refuse to let them escape. We deceive ourselves, though, as well as cheat the people we categorise. This remark about women, after all, shows that the *male speaker himself*, not the women he accuses, is unable or unwilling to argue rationally! Prejudices tell us more about the speaker than about those who are described.

Unfortunately, though, prejudices can be self-fulfilling. Suppose that a police officer in Brixton believes that more black youths than white youths are likely to be thieves. Naturally, the officer will stop and search more blacks than whites. If the two groups were, in fact, *equally* likely to be criminals, the very method of investigation would result in more blacks than whites being arrested. Future statistics would then misleadingly authenticate the false belief, and would appear to justify the original racist assumption.

A second example concerns Britain's class structure. A few years ago I came across an enormous book which seemed to date from the first decade of this century. It was entitled *The Ideal Home: How to Find it, How to Furnish*

it, How to Keep it, and was written by Matilda Lees-Dods
– Diplomée of the National Training School of Cookery,
South Kensington, Certified Teacher in Laundry Work,
Dressmaking, Dairy Work, Poultry Rearing and First Aid –
impressive credentials indeed! She advises,

> Domestics, many or few, must be up and doing at early
> and fixed hours. No greater aid to this, and no greater
> boon to the other domestics, is there than the order
> that a cup of tea, whether required or not, should be
> served to the lady of the house at 7.30 . . . The mistress
> with the knowledge that all her domestics are up and
> at work has her last hour in bed converted into a time
> of genuine rest.

It is impossible not to wonder about the practical effects
of a world-view which attributes to the middle classes delic-
ate nerves, the need for a regular lie-in, and the stressful
duty of ensuring that the servants are safely at work from
shortly after dawn.

Prejudice comes easily to us, partly because of the very
structure of our minds. We can scarcely even think about
anyone we know without using 'category words', which
focus on some selected aspect of the person, while temporarily excluding from our attention other aspects which may
be no less important. A young woman will be viewed quite
differently by different people, according to *their* interests.
Her employer may see her as a high achiever, her small
sister as a protector, her boyfriend's parents as a spendthrift.
But these categories are not self-contained. No one is *simply*
a 'capitalist', a 'criminal', or even an 'adult' or a 'Christian'.
The danger of abstractions (which we cannot do without in
order to think at all) is that they can blind us to the com-
plexity and richness of human experience: then, in the
words of William Wordsworth, 'we murder to dissect'.

We can even afflict ourselves in this way. People whose
marriage has broken down, for example, may think of themselves for years as 'divorced' or 'separated' people. Obvi-

ously, these terms have their truth, for such experiences, and the suffering that comes with them, mark people deeply and determine many of their continuing circumstances and preoccupations. But to *define* oneself by such a label is to be locked into the past, and to be less free to face the future.

We could rightly ask what kind of relationship with others is possible when we take this kind of attitude. In a way, though, that question misses the point. Prejudice often functions, whether consciously or not, precisely to enforce the power of a social group. It labels other groups of people inferior in some way, and presumes that this supposed inferiority is the decisive truth about them. In this way it licences us to ignore their words, rights and feelings, and dispenses us from building a serious relationship with them.

In the gospel of John (1:46), when the apostle Philip mentions Jesus to Nathanael, Nathanael replies, 'From Nazareth? Can anything good come from that place?'. In Northern Ireland, some people say, to ask strangers 'What school were you at?' is the quickest way to learn which religious group they belong to, and so to learn the 'correct' response of friendliness or hostility. An officer in a remand prison once said to me, 'You know, Father, what we're dealing with here is ninety per cent rubbish'.

In our story of Jane and Susan, the insulting phrase 'mental cases' works in this way. It exposes the speaker's bias, invites Jane to share it, and, most importantly, it rules out any possible welcome for the people (not 'the cases') so described. It is likely, of course, that money is a strong (if unadmitted) motive for those opposing the hostel. Local property values are at risk. But the very fact of that risk would only show that modern society is no less subject to taboos than first-century Palestine. That a blind fear is indeed at work is suggested by the abnormal force of Susan's anger when Jane challenges her.

Confronting such powerful biases, as Jane does, needs courage. At the same time, the excessive reaction shows how effective and worthwhile the challenge is. Prejudice flourishes best when left unexamined, as Jesus points out:

'. . . everybody who does wrong
hates the light and avoids it,
to prevent his actions
   from being shown up;
but whoever does the truth
comes out into the light,
so that what he is doing
   may plainly appear as done in God.'
(John 3:20–1)

FOR REFLECTION

1. It might be interesting to collect a week's issues of your usual daily newspaper, and then to go through the set. Which groups (e.g. political parties, occupational or racial groups), are consistently attacked or scorned? Can you recall the paper *ever* praising them. If not, what does this suggest about the newspaper itself?
2. Are you aware of having grown out of some prejudice which you once held? How did the prejudice take hold, and what led to your being freed from it?
3. Can you think of any types of people who would feel unwelcome in your local parish? How is this sense of rejection created?

PRAYER

Lord Jesus, you are the light which darkness cannot over-power. We ask that we may be released from our areas of blindness and prejudice, so that we come to see ourselves and all other people by your light; with openness, respect and compassion.

Refusing to Forget

❐

JACKIE AND KEVIN had sat in the Welfare Office for more than two hours. Though the baby on Jackie's knee had started to cry, they twice let other people go ahead of them in the queue. When they finally approached one of the counter staff, you could see what an effort it cost them. In the interview room, their story began hesitantly, then spilled out all at once.

'I suppose I've been drinking too much for years, ever since I lost my job', said Kevin. 'A couple of times, I've come in from the pub and knocked Jackie about. No broken bones, you know, bruises, but I felt terrible afterwards, especially once when she was pregnant with Kim. I've told her never again, I've promised. But I'm scared it might carry on and get worse.'

Jackie broke in, tears in her eyes. 'That's not the real reason we've come, though. Last week I hit the baby. I'd never done that before. She'd been crying for hours and I just lost my temper. Kevin wasn't at home, but I had to tell him. We didn't know what to do, and I just couldn't admit it to my mum. In the end I told my auntie, and she said to come in here. We weren't sure whether to come. You hear all these stories about social workers taking children into care, and we really love Kim. But that's the reason why we're here.'

❐

Yahweh said to Moses, 'Tell the Israelites this . . . "You

will not spread false rumours. You will not lend support to
the wicked by giving untrue evidence. You will not be led
into wrong-doing by the majority nor, when giving evidence
in a lawsuit, side with the majority to pervert the course
of justice; nor will you show partiality to the poor in a
lawsuit.

"If you come on your enemy's ox or donkey straying, you
will take it back to him. If you see the donkey of someone
who hates you fallen under its load, do not stand back;
you must go and help him with it.

"You will not cheat the poor among you of their rights
at law. Keep clear of fraud. Do not cause the death of the
innocent or upright, and do not acquit the guilty. You will
accept no bribes, for a bribe blinds the clear-sighted and is
the ruin of the cause of the upright.

"You will not oppress the alien; you know how an alien
feels, for you yourselves were once aliens in Egypt." '

(Exodus 20:22; 23:1–9)

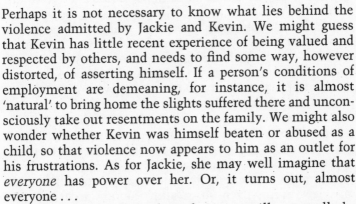

Perhaps it is not necessary to know what lies behind the
violence admitted by Jackie and Kevin. We might guess
that Kevin has little recent experience of being valued and
respected by others, and needs to find some way, however
distorted, of asserting himself. If a person's conditions of
employment are demeaning, for instance, it is almost
'natural' to bring home the slights suffered there and uncon-
sciously take out resentments on the family. We might also
wonder whether Kevin was himself beaten or abused as a
child, so that violence now appears to him as an outlet for
his frustrations. As for Jackie, she may well imagine that
everyone has power over her. Or, it turns out, almost
everyone . . .

Neither need we know how their case will eventually be
resolved. What the story does is record a potential turning
point. Instead of keeping what has happened secret, and
even trying to forget it themselves, Jackie and Kevin have
taken the risk of exposing their shame to scrutiny. The very

act of coming to the office for help shows them putting Kim's welfare before their own 'right to privacy'. Their attitude to each other, too, is fundamentally generous. It would have been easy for them to have blamed each other, or pleaded the pressure of their external circumstances, such as shortage of money and the tensions it brings. Probably, as the situation is worked through, some of that excusing of self will emerge. But their first move is to shoulder personal responsibility. To that extent they accept, not reject, each other. What inspires their tentative (but maybe decisive) step forward, it appears, is a courageous willingness to stay in touch with their own pain – and with their own capacity to inflict pain. The positive force behind their search for healing is not forgetting but *remembering*.

What goes for personal relationships applies also to public life. In Eastern Europe and in Soviet Central Asia, we have recently seen the re-emergence of bitter and 'traditional' ethnic conflicts. Up to a point, it had proved possible to impose a temporary political unity on diverse and conflicting cultures. The ethnic or national differences were discounted or presumed to be no longer relevant, because significance was officially attributed only to a supposed communist unity. Therefore, profound mutual grievances were systematically buried (as it were, officially 'forgotten'), and could not be examined or discussed openly. As soon as the centralised authority loosened, renewed clashes were probably inevitable.

Naturally, not every act of memory has a healing effect. It is possible to destroy one's own peace of spirit by nursing resentments for years, awaiting the chance for some satisfying act of revenge, meanwhile taking every small opportunity to damage an enemy: as the saying goes, 'Don't get mad, get even'. Even so, healing cannot occur *without* memory. In Jewish spirituality, as it happens, the link between memory and healing is explicit. The Hebrew term *teshuvah*, which means roughly 'conversion', has been explained by Rabbi Leon Klenicki, as follows: '*Teshuvah* is a reconsideration of the past towards a transformation of the heart, a reconsideration of past events and even present realities'. He himself goes on to suggest that such a 'change of heart' (and nothing less) is needed for Jewish dialogue with the Christian Churches. Through *'teshuvah'*, Jews might recognise, accept, and respond to Christians' repentance for the long history of their oppression of Jews. Similarly, in the Book of Exodus as a whole, there survives considerable resentment towards Egypt. But what is central in the key passage quoted above is the lesson *Israel itself* must learn from its memory of suffering.

The structure of this passage is as important as its content. A series of practices which promote or corrupt the general good is listed. One must not destroy others' reputations, must respect the humanity of opponents without seeking to harm them, must not 'pervert the cause of justice'. What is far more difficult than identifying good and evil, though, is finding the shared motivation to pursue the goods stated, and avoid the evils.

Take one example which Exodus clearly considers crucial, that of the law. We speak of 'Justices of the Peace', of the 'Lord Chief Justice', of the 'scales of justice', and so on. Such expressions emphasise our shared yearning that the law should, indeed, dispense justice. Yet it is plain that not everyone who is brought to court is brought to justice. (Think of the cases of the 'Birmingham Six' and the 'Guildford Four'.) Even at their best, courts can only *apply* the law, not determine which laws are passed in the first place; and we can all think of witticisms which express a widespread awareness that laws do not impartially serve the common good. As Anatole France wrote in the nineteenth century, 'the law in its majestic equality forbids the rich as well as the poor to sleep under bridges, to beg in the streets, and to steal bread'. Again, we recognise the ideal of 'equality before the law', and might even suppose that in our own legal system the ideal is realised. The powerful know better. The American financier J. P. Morgan boasted that he employed lawyers not to tell him what he couldn't do, but to make it legal when he did it! Or as the poet Robert Frost put a similar point, a jury consists of twelve persons chosen to decide who has the better lawyer. The more plausible we believe such remarks to be, the less we shall enjoy their wit.

Contempt for the law would be no remedy for its abuse. In a state of lawlessness, the weak would certainly suffer no less than they do under the law. Nevertheless, it is a kind of superstition, of magical thinking, to assume that the outer forms of law ensure the practice of justice. The question is, *how* can the law be made to defend, not pervert, 'the cause of justice'? Legal systems do not come down from heaven, but are rooted in the values of a given society. If, for example, a majority of the British Parliament is hostile to immigrants, any Immigration Act it passes will reflect that hostility. It would, indeed, be worth considering this Act in the light of the phrase, 'You know how an alien feels, for you yourselves were once aliens in Egypt'. In Exodus it is this very declaration which underpins the specific commands and prohibitions which are to govern the social order. It implies that you cannot truly experience injustice, poverty, ruthlessness, or abuse of the legal system (and therefore you cannot begin to set such evils right) until you 'remember' what it is to be a victim.

Much social injustice may derive from a particular type of stupidity, the stupidity of those who are intellectually gifted but have lost touch with the life going on around them. Not long ago a senior government minister, speaking within his own field of responsibility, declared that there was no poverty in the United Kingdom. The reaction to his statement was so strong that he was dismissed from his post soon after. His claim could be interpreted in several ways. It means, obviously, that the minister was not himself *aware* of poverty. Secondly, it functions as a disguised statement of policy, since there is no need to seek remedies for what one says does not exist. But it also claims to describe the situation objectively. In this last respect, the Minister's statement contradicted the immediate experience of millions. Apart from the destitute, who sleep under bridges in

winter (just as in Anatole France's day) or bring up their
children in 'Bed and Breakfast' hostels, there are far larger
numbers who live in 'ordinary' grinding poverty. That is,
they have no money for presents, holidays, school trips,
visits to relatives, and so on. There are many others, such
as district nurses, social workers, and some teachers and
doctors, who are not poor themselves but who retain close
personal or professional contact with the poor.

But from his very different perspective, the minister was,
indeed, *not aware* of poverty. In this respect he was oblivi-
ous, in a stupor – 'stupid'. There is little to be gained by
accusing one politician, even if one could make the accusation stick. He represents the kind of failure in perception
which threatens everyone. All of us are capable of stupidity,
because we all sometimes cultivate certain areas of ignorance, at least half-deliberately, to safeguard our peace of
mind. Most British newspapers, for instance, distort their
coverage of violence in Northern Ireland by omitting any
serious discussion of the long-standing violence and dis-
crimination suffered by the religious and political minority.
We hear little, similarly, of the violence which ethnic minorities consistently experience in, say, London's East End.
Of the violence in places like East Timor and Guatemala
we get virtually no news at all. Such self-censorship, or
'news management', might amount to 'propaganda' if it
served the interests of powerful groups who wanted us to
know as little as possible about a given situation and its
causes. But more often than not, probably, the papers simply
assume our lack of interest. If we *really* wanted fuller and
more balanced information about Northern Ireland than the
tabloids print, we could find it without much trouble. No
one, admittedly, can take on the world's burdens single-
handed, and it is useless to feel guilt at failing to respond
to each one of the never-ending crises and tragedies which
come to our attention. But what would it indicate if we
were interested in *no* such matters?

Jackie and Kevin cannot resolve their shared desperation
till they face their pain together. The Israelites could not

realistically plan for a just society without calling to mind their former oppression. We cannot act against the injustices or the violence of our own society until we allow ourselves to be troubled by them, until we find some way of 'staying in touch' with their victims. The next chapter will consider one way in which this insight has recently influenced the Church's understanding of itself.

FOR REFLECTION

1. Does the saying 'forgive and forget' make sense? Or is it closer to the truth to say that, if we are to forgive, we need to 'remember' what has hurt us and how it has affected us? What would distinguish this act of remembering from the destructive act of nursing a grievance?
2. How might people in power remain in touch with those whom their decisions might damage most severely?
3. Is it possible to enable politicians, for example, to admit mistakes without necessarily forfeiting the respect of others? Or does the party system in Britain condemn politicians to an automatic and unceasing public attack on their opponents?

PRAYER

Our being holds no secrets from you, Lord, and our own assumptions about our innocence can never justify us in your sight. Through your Holy Spirit, give us courage to remain open to people who disturb us and to realities which we would prefer to ignore. Give us, too, a passion for truth which alerts us to those whose interests tempt them to deceive themselves and us. We do not seek to become judges of one another, but to learn a deeper unity with all your people. We make this prayer in the name of Jesus, your son and the brother of us all.

The Standpoint of the Poor

A YEAR AGO, Mary was diagnosed HIV Positive. It seemed she had contracted the virus through her boyfriend, Dave, who had had a relationship with someone who was infected. Her first reaction was one of shock, her second was of desperate fear. She assumed that she was already terminally ill with AIDS, or at least that it was only briefly dormant within her and she would soon die.

Later she was swamped with guilt. The papers had been full of tragic stories that Eastern European babies, 'innocent victims', had contracted AIDS through infected blood transfusions. Compared with these cases, Mary's condition was self-inflicted, and she couldn't help blaming herself. Also, though she no longer attended church, she still thought of herself as 'half a Catholic'. She found herself imagining that her plight was some kind of punishment for sin. People she thought of as pious talked of AIDS as a 'gay plague' which had nothing to do with those who 'lived a moral life'. Mary's own mother, who had once bitterly accused Mary of promiscuity, gave her little support. Her mother talked about feeling 'dirty', especially since Mary had told a few family friends about the diagnosis. She wouldn't let Dave in the house, saying that Mary's determination not to split up with him just proved she had no shame.

Mary often felt overwhelmed by fear of what would happen, to Dave as well as to herself. At these times, the combination of fear and guilt made her life seem futile and hopeless. Strangely, though, she found herself groping towards a new way of looking at her life. For years, without asking herself why, she had felt vaguely dissatisfied. She supposed she had expected the itch to be soothed by extra money, more nights out, more popularity, more friends. Now she was able to admit to herself that she had been jealous of Dave's friendships, half assuming that when it suited him he would abandon her and move on. But gradually after their diagnosis, their relationship grew much deeper so that its importance in Mary's life outweighed all that she had lost and might lose. Dave had lost his job, and hers was neither demanding nor interesting, so they had plenty of time to go for walks and listen to music and just be together. Mary had a new sense that each day was a gift, whatever the future might bring. As someone said to her, the point is not death itself, but the manner of a person's living and dying. In the end, no one gets out alive!

<hr />

He [Jesus] . . . set out for the territory of Tyre. There he went into a house and did not want anyone to know he was there; but he could not pass unrecognised. At once a woman whose little daughter had an unclean spirit heard about him and came and fell at his feet. Now this woman was a gentile, by birth a Syro-Phoenician, and she begged him to drive the devil out of her daughter. And he said to her, 'The children should be fed first, because it is not fair to take the children's food and throw it to little dogs'. But she spoke up, 'Ah yes, sir,' she replied, 'but little dogs under the table eat the scraps from the children.' And he said to her, 'For saying this you may go home happy; the devil has gone out of your daughter.' So she went off home and found the child lying on the bed and the devil gone.

(Mark 7:24–30)

<hr />

This is an astonishing story. In the gospel of Mark, Jesus's disciples are consistently represented as dim at best, deeply resistant to his message at worst. In contrast, Jesus is sometimes gentle and sometimes fierce, but always full of wisdom and integrity. His decisive sayings tend to settle all disputes. (In fact, the stories often seem designed precisely to highlight such punchlines.) Similarly, he is never defeated in argument by his powerful civil and religious opponents. But the gospel gives us this one exceptional story of someone who argues with Jesus – and wins!

It is intriguing to consider what might underlie this surprise. In other stories, Jesus usually stands as an 'outsider', challenging the enormous weight of the disciples' ingrained assumptions or confronting the self-interest which was built into the religious system of Galilee and Judaea (as it is into all religious and social systems). But here in this story, and perhaps only here, he appears as the one *with privilege*, the one who himself needs to be challenged. A gentile woman, and probably a poor one, fits the bill, since these factors alone would, in that society, mark her as someone of little account. But in addition, she is the mother of an unclean daughter whom she evidently refuses to abandon, with the result that she herself becomes unclean in the eyes of the devout. She is also a Canaanite, a Syro-Phoenician, one who belonged to a culture that was thought to endanger the purity of Israel's faith. (The best known Phoenician woman in the Bible is Jezebel, whom the Bible rarely mentions without disgust.)

Daringly, Mark's gospel here presents Jesus as grudging, even hostile. His use of the image of the children and the dogs amounts to an insult. Nervous Christian interpreters tend to suggest that Jesus is 'testing' the woman, or that the exchange shows that he has, after all, a sense of humour. These explanations do not help, since they imply that Jesus would willingly manipulate or tease a person who was suffering desperately. It seems preferable to admit that Jesus for once exhibits a deficient sense of the scope of his own purpose. It is the Canaanite woman who recalls him to the richness and the universal mission of prophetic Judaism.

The story has a double significance. We are shown that Jesus, because he is fully human, has to learn as he goes along. Like all of us, he is formed and taught by others. Secondly, and equally important, we notice that he opens himself to the influence of someone whom others would reject automatically. She is the poor person who mourns, and who is blessed in her mournings (see Luke 6:20–6). Even when she enters into dialogue with Jesus himself, there is no standpoint better than hers!

Every society drives certain groups of people to its margin. Such groups may be racial, tribal or religious minorities. They may be the sick, the aged or the mentally ill, who must depend on others for their care. Numerically speaking they may not be 'minorities' at all, as when economic or political power is concentrated in a very few hands and the masses are virtually dispossessed. The Syro-Phoenician woman teaches us that the insight of those excluded from the social mainstream, even when they are in the ordinary sense uneducated or 'ignorant', may be more penetrating than that of people who are settled, comfortable and widely respected.

For example, at the heart of our modern Western culture is an optimistic assumption about 'progress'. The word crops up everywhere, as a description or as a promise; in the language of politicians, journalists, business executives, advertisers. In some ways, certainly, progress seems so undeniable as to call for our gratitude. Visits to the dentist, for example, no longer cause terror, and dental services have been made available to almost everyone. But 'progress' always comes with a price-tag. What brings benefits to some can plunge others into hardship, such as when new industrial technology leads to many people losing their jobs, or when agricultural developments make small farms uneconomic. Even in the case of dentistry, the cost of progress means it is possible that many people will in future be unable to afford dental treatment, as is now the case in the USA. 'Progress' *as such*, therefore, is not a concept that makes sense. We always need to ask 'progress for whom?', or 'progress in what way?'. For a rounded assessment of progress we need to consult those who are its victims, those whom we call, in shorthand, 'the poor'.

'Poverty' in this sense is not simply a shortage of money, though shortage of money will usually be at its heart. It is marked by a range of experiences; of being disregarded, or excluded, or despised, or oppressed. Industrial workers may be able, for example, through a strong trade union, to negotiate a fair pay deal; if united, workers can have a definite but restricted power. But the unemployed are in no position to negotiate the level of their benefit. They are 'poor': powerless, primarily, but almost certainly short of money too. Mary, in our story, would be 'poor' in this broader sense even if she had no urgent money worries, since her dominant experience is that of being rejected and condemned, not respected. And yet it is on the basis of this very experience that she discovers value in what others overlook or can't be bothered with. Her angle of vision allows her to find a new truth, to receive a new gift of the Spirit.

What has come to be called in Church circles the 'preferential option for the poor' can be seen as an attempt on the part of Christians to *learn from outsiders*, as Jesus learns from the Canaanite woman. The Church has always professed a concern for the poor, and has, at its best, acted vigorously out of this concern. But those who have made policy in the Church, and those who have most influenced its intellectual life, have seldom been in close touch with poverty. Where Church life has been controlled by the clergy, their training has tended to lift out of poverty even those among them who once knew it. Where lay-persons have been more influential (as, for example, where parishes of the Church of England fell within the patronage of the gentry), this influence has belonged overwhelmingly to a social elite. Accordingly, the problem of poverty has been defined, and the responses to it prescribed, by those whose good will may be admirable, but whose experience is second-hand.

Typically, social concern has been expressed through 'works of charity'. Works of charity will always be needed.

But 'charity', or 'philanthropy', expresses the mind of the donors not the recipients. It is possible for 'works of charity' to be tainted at their source, which can mean they do as much harm as good. They might, for example, confirm the donors in a false sense of their own virtue, and give the recipients an equally false sense of their own helplessness; or they might be taken as evidence that justice is unnecessary, since the prosperous can be counted on to be 'charitable'. According to the distinguished American theologian Reinhold Niebuhr, philanthropy unites the expression of pity with the retention of power. To the philanthropist, the poor are *objects of concern*. As soon as they begin to assert themselves, assistance is likely to be indignantly withdrawn. The 'option for the poor' seeks to overcome this limitation by *making the perspective of the poor of primary importance*.

In his famous book *Pedagogy of the Oppressed* the Brazilian educator Paulo Freire puts the matter this way: in a situation of massive injustice, it is likely that some privileged people will courageously throw in their lot with the oppressed:

> Theirs is a fundamental role, and has been so throughout the history of this struggle. It happens, however, that as they cease to be exploiters or indifferent spectators or simply the heirs of exploitation and move to the side of the exploited, they almost always bring with them the marks of their origin: their prejudices and their deformations, which include a lack of confidence in the people's ability to think, to want, and to know . . . [Such converts] truly desire to transform the unjust order; but because of their background they believe that they must be the executors of the transformation. They talk about the people, but they do not trust them . . .

By the same token, the Church's 'option for the poor' is not primarily a decision to give priority to the poor as it dispenses its pastoral services. Nor is it a recommendation that sincere Christians should flee the suburbs and flood local authorities with demands for council flats (though the Church cannot afford to be absent from such places, or to ignore what it learns there). Rather, it is a recognition that the Church, like Jesus himself, must *allow itself to be decisively influenced* by the experience of the poor. A faithful response to this call would transform Church life in ways we can now hardly anticipate.

'To trust the people': the phrase sounds both straightforward and unrealistic. The poor, like anyone else, are not exempt from stupidity or selfishness or greed. Nor must we assume that rich people are vicious or blind, or that 'middle-class' expertise is irrelevant. (We would not wish Mary to be without skilled medical or psychological attention, for example.) But it remains true that the poor might be free from some of the illusions which in our Western culture threaten the affluent and the satisfied – not least among members of the Church: illusions such as the sense that we don't need saving, because we can take care of ourselves; that a competitive world in which everyone must fend for themselves can produce a society that is responsive to the most urgent and basic human needs; that we can do good to others without being changed ourselves; that hardship and failure cannot be endured; that the successful deserve special attention, and the feeble may reasonably be overlooked.

FOR REFLECTION

1. Think back to an occasion when you seemed to acquire some new vision or insight. Are you aware what situation, what struggle, what relationship prepared you for it?

2. Consider a remark of the nineteenth-century Scottish Protestant writer, George Macdonald: 'What riches and fancied religion, with the self-sufficiency they generate between them, can make a man or woman capable of,

is appalling . . . To many of the religious rich, the great damning revelation will be their behaviour to the poor to whom they thought themselves very kind.' In what sense might 'kindness' be destructive?
3. Does it make sense to talk about the poor being 'blessed' and at the same time work hard to lessen poverty?
4. How might the Church respond helpfully to the needs of those who are HIV Positive, or who are suffering from AIDS? What might Christians have to learn from them?

PRAYER

Lord God, Jesus your son lived among us, shared our weakness and became our brother. In this way he gave you glory and made your Kingdom present among us. May we learn to give generously to one another and receive joyously from one another. May we all be united in the Spirit who can fill us with wisdom and love.

Home Truths?

RACHEL AND DAVID had two children; Julia was six and John four. They lived in South London, where Rachel had recently become more and more involved in the local Justice and Peace Group.

This Group had decided to respond to the increasing problem of youth homelessness by converting part of the parish hall into a day centre, where people in need could come for tea, sandwiches and a chat. Now that Julia was at school and John was old enough to go to nursery school, Rachel felt free to do some work at the centre. Occasionally, in order to work her shift, she had to collect the children from school and bring them with her to the day centre for a couple of hours.

Rachel's commitment to the centre was causing considerable tension at home. Her parents had been upset when they'd heard Julia use a four-letter word – correctly and in context! Sometimes Rachel brought home some fairly filthy laundry to wash, and she once had to cancel a long-anticipated night out at the theatre with David because of a sudden crisis at the day centre. Then, one day, she came home with a young man who looked in a bad way; dirty, haggard, smelling of drink. She explained that he had nowhere to stay. She'd agreed to let him have the spare room for the night, and planned to take him to the doctor for a check-up next morning.

David was furious. He said he'd had enough. 'You know I'm up to my neck at work, and I think I've the right to a

bit of peace and quiet when I come home. I don't like finding
this yob with his feet up on the couch while you make him
a slap-up meal. You don't know anything about the guy! I
don't care what you do, but I won't have the kids put at
risk just because you think you can solve the homelessness
problem single-handed. Why can't you think of your own
family for once?'

*He [Jesus] went home again, and once more such a crowd
collected that they could not even have a meal. When his
relations heard of this, they set out to take charge of him;
they said, 'He is out of his mind.' ...*

*Now his mother and his brothers arrived and, standing
outside, sent in a message asking for him. A crowd was
sitting round him at the time the message was passed to
him, 'Look, your mother and brothers and sisters are outside asking for you.' He replied, 'Who are my mother and
my brothers?' And looking at those sitting in a circle round
him, he said, 'Here are my mother and my brothers.
Anyone who does the will of God, that person is my brother
and sister and mother.' ...*

*'Look,' [Peter said to Jesus], 'we have left everything and
followed you.' Jesus said, 'In truth, I tell you, there is no
one who has left house, brothers, sisters, mother, father,
children or land for my sake and for the sake of the gospel
who will not receive a hundred times as much, houses,
brothers, sisters, mothers, children and land – and persecutions too – now in this present time and, in the world
to come, eternal life. Many who are first will be last, and
the last, first.'*

(Mark 3:20–1, 31–5; 10:28–31)

The gospels often indicate that Jesus was hard on families.
In Mark's account of the call of the first disciples (1:16–20),
Simon and Andrew leave their nets to follow Jesus – with-
out a word of explanation to anyone. James and John simply

leave their father Zebedee in the boat, and clear off. There go the family's future bread-winners! How can they now fulfil the commandment to 'Honour your father and your mother', since that commandment means at least supporting them when they grow old? In Matthew 8:21-2, Jesus seems even more ruthless. A would-be disciple asks 'Lord, let me go and bury my father first', to which Jesus replies, 'Follow me, and let the dead bury their dead'. This saying must have shocked Jesus's hearers and Matthew's readers deeply: and it must have been *meant* to shock. It runs counter to our most basic sense of decency and piety. Who would willingly fail to bury a parent? In Luke 11:27-8, to someone who calls out 'Blessed the womb that bore you and the breasts that fed you', Jesus replies, 'More blessed still are those who hear the word of God and keep it'. Luke also gives us the story of Jesus in the Temple (2:41-50), in which, even as a child, Jesus makes it clear that his work entails breaking sharply with his parents and their assumptions. As the gospel concedes, they cannot understand this; and we can't help sympathising.

These sayings do not amount to a *rejection* of the family. Family members, like anyone else, are blessed when they 'hear the word of God and keep it'. But it does seem that Jesus brings into question *the claims* of the family. Without good friends, and especially without those who have nurtured us and still share our lives most intimately, we would shrivel. We have to thank God for the gift of these relationships and sustain them in our turn. We can never simply shrug off our responsibility to our families. But family loyalties often have to compete with other demands. A job, for instance, may require extensive overtime, frequent periods away from home, or unsocial hours. Certainly, we ought to ensure, if possible, that we do not neglect family and friends, and perhaps some jobs ought to be reorganised so that family life is not sacrificed. Presumably, for example, one reason why there are so few women in the House of Commons is the hours MPs are expected to work, and the comparative absence of women in Parliament may well seriously detract from the quality of our politics. Meanwhile, though, in the absence of reform, the tension experienced by MPs cannot automatically be resolved in favour of the needs of their families.

In his autobiography, *And There Was Light* the French philosopher Jacques Lusseyran, who was totally blind from the age of seven, tells of an extreme experience of cruelly divided loyalties. When he was only sixteen he had a key role in the French Resistance. He still lived at home but, because informers were everywhere, he had to keep his Resistance involvement absolutely secret: above all from his family, since any gossip and any over-anxiety on their part would give him away immediately. In a terrible sense, his enemies were those of his own household. Jesus insists that the Kingdom of God must come first: but these tough sayings seem to recognise how hard it is to put the Kingdom first when it is often our closest relationships which comprise our main competing loyalty.

Another point to note is this: any genuine gift has its dark side. Without a loving and reasonably stable upbringing, it is far more difficult to become a mature, free and spontaneous adult. But families can also stifle freedom. In our story, we can assume that Rachel enjoys being a wife and mother. But those labels can also be used to define her as a person, to deny that she has interests, rights, obligations of her own. A number of people believe that a wife's true role is that of accessory to her husband and children, with no life apart from theirs: her proper tasks are those which meet their domestic or emotional needs. To live the gospel, and indeed simply to mature as a person, she may well have to rebel against these conventional expectations, to recognise commitments beyond, as well as within, the family unit: and these outside commitments may sometimes need to be put first.

To be a parent is to accept the task of caring lovingly for one's children. But this by no means implies that society's conventional notions of what it is to be 'well brought-up' are adequate. Is it really always in the true interests of children to be protected from all the suffering and pain of the world around them? Must Rachel, to be a 'good mother', hide the poor from her children and her children from the poor?

The traditional Western idea of the family is of a more or less self-contained unit, a tranquil refuge from the tough world outside. Think of the old song 'Home, Sweet Home'. In 'the world', we tend to suppose, those who try to 'love their neighbour' are just asking to be exploited and victimised; but within the family, harmony and love are somehow 'natural' and conflicts are 'unnatural'. This attitude, which separates the welfare of one's family from that of the outside world, cheapens the meaning of 'love' and of 'home'. We can make no sense of the teaching of Jesus unless we accept that love is possible in the wider world. On the other hand, loving-kindness is no more 'natural' within the family than it is anywhere else. In fact, where we love most we are likely to face the deepest and most painful conflicts. The more we are sentimental about family life, the more likely it is that real life will lead us to reject what we have sentimentalised. In *this* sense of the word 'home', the words of the song need adapting: 'There's no place like home – not even home'.

What goes for families also goes for larger social units. The more close-knit a group becomes, the more it resists challenge in the name of a more universal good. Under Hitler, the interests of the Nazis were claimed to be identical with the interests of Germany, even with the interests of 'civilisation'. Those outside the Nazi movement who threatened it in any way (Jews especially, on grounds of race, but also communists, say, on political grounds) could be labelled as demonic, as the source of all evil, and could therefore be crushed without qualm.

There are less dramatic examples, closer to home. In some countries there grows up a kind of 'police culture'. Children will follow parents into the police force, a policeman will marry the sister of a colleague. There is a healthy phenomenon in so far as people doing a tough job are helped by receiving the understanding and the support they need. But such intimacy, such 'inbreeding', means that the group will tend to close ranks under pressure and to keep out recruits who jeopardise its unity. It can even be tempted to cover up for colleagues who have acted unjustly or unlawfully. A similar sectional interest and defensiveness can surface in a religious order or a bench of bishops, a trade union or employers' organisation or professional association. In fact, any group closely bonded by class or economic status, by race, profession or religious belief, can put its own preservation and welfare above all other considerations. Under challenge, the main principle of action can shrink to a cry of 'Repel boarders', or 'Don't rock the boat'. Usually, the sin of exclusiveness will be falsely dignified with the name of some good quality it perverts: 'loyalty', 'solidarity', 'comradeship', *esprit de corps*, 'cabinet responsibility'. But the Kingdom of God is intended for all, and can admit no cliques.

In her autobiography *An American Childhood*, Annie Dillard recalls her affluent Presbyterian upbringing, and marvels at the way that Sunday School instruction tamed the Bible. She writes of 'the dense and staggering texts they read us placidly, sweet-mouthed and earnest, week after week'. Then she goes on,

> Why did they spread this scandalous document before our eyes? If they had read it, I thought, they would have hid it. They didn't recognise the vivid danger that we would, through repeated exposure, catch a case of its wild opposition to their world. Instead they bade us study great chunks of it, and think about those chunks, and commit them to memory, and ignore them. By dipping us children in the Bible so often, they hoped, I think, to give our lives a serious tint, and to provide us with magnificent snatches of prayer to produce as charms . . .

But if the Scriptures leave us undisturbed, we cannot be reading them attentively enough.

FOR REFLECTION

1. If Rachel or David confided in you about their argument, how might you respond?
2. Can you think of ways in which you have felt you must defy or oppose your family or closest friends, without at all wishing to reject them? Were such actions *interpreted* as rejection?
3. Do you sometimes find yourself expecting that the people closest to you must, above all, meet your own needs or expectations?

PRAYER

Lord, I thank you for those people who are closest to me. Teach me to love them more fully, to leave them free to live up to their own convictions with courage, as I would wish to do myself. May we together seek for our true tasks in life and for our deepest good. We ask this through our brother Jesus, and through the power of his Spirit.

Under Judgment

❖━━❖

As PARISH PRIEST, Father Conroy chaired the Board of
Governors of the local Catholic school. Mrs Murphy, Head
of Religious Education in the school, had recently become
interested in the position of women in the Church. Father
Conroy was disturbed at this. During one Governor's meeting he had strongly criticised her for devoting a series of
sixth-form classes to 'sexist language' in prayer and liturgy,
the limited scope for women's ministry, and the history of
Christian attitudes towards women. Her job was to teach
the fundamentals of faith, he argued, not to go overboard
on the latest fashionable ideas. She had been defended by
others at the meeting, and Father Conroy had let the matter
drop.

Mrs Murphy also belonged to the parish Justice and Peace
group. At her suggestion, the group decided to consider
the implications of feminism for the local church. They
organised a study day and arranged for an outside speaker,
a woman theologian who lectured at the University. The
group usually met in the presbytery, but on this occasion
Father Conroy told them they would not be welcome to do
so. He also declined to publicise the event in the parish
newsletter. He said he thought that the meeting would
reinforce divisions within the parish and, in any case, that
the issue was irrelevant to the parish's real needs. There
were far more urgent issues of justice that deserved their
attention. Certainly the parish had subsidised Justice and
Peace gatherings before, paying such expenses as speakers'

travel, but he could not consider this particular event to be a proper use of church funds.

<><>

Then addressing the crowds and the disciples Jesus said, 'The scribes and the Pharisees occupy the chair of Moses. You must therefore do and observe what they tell you; but do not be guided by what they do, since they do not practise what they preach. They tie up heavy burdens and lay them on people's shoulders, but will they lift a finger to move them? Not they! Everything they do is done to attract attention, like wearing broader headbands and longer tassels, like wanting to take the place of honour at banquets and the front seats in the synagogues, being greeted respectfully in the market squares and having people call them Rabbi.

'You, however, must not allow yourselves to be called Rabbi, since you have only one Master, and you are all brothers. You must call no one on earth your father, since you have only one Father, and he is in heaven. Nor must you allow yourselves to be called teachers, for you have only one Teacher, the Christ. The greatest among you must be your servant. Anyone who raises himself up will be humbled, and anyone who humbles himself will be raised up.

'Alas for you, scribes and Pharisees, you hypocrites! You shut up the kingdom of Heaven in people's faces, neither going in yourselves nor allowing others to go in who want to.'

(Matthew 23:1–13)

<><>

No major religious body is without its divisions. The gospels often refer to the contrast between the Pharisees' belief and practice and that of the aristocratic priestly group, the Sadducees, who ran the Jerusalem Temple. By the time the gospel of Matthew was written the Temple had been destroyed, and the power of the Sadducees along with it. The Pharisees were better placed to survive this catastrophe.

They were a lay group, who held the noble ideal of allowing their faith in God to affect the whole of their everyday lives. They would have echoed Jeremiah's severe criticism of any religion which put its trust in formal worship alone (see Jeremiah 7:1–15). So their primary concern was shared with Jesus and his followers.

It is significant, for instance, that Acts 23:6–9 tells us that Paul takes their side against the Sadducees, calling himself 'a Pharisee and the son of a Pharisee'. Jesus, too, often eats with them and must have been regarded in the popular mind as a Pharisee himself. In Luke 13:31, it is friendly Pharisees who come to warn Jesus that Herod means to kill him. Even the constant disputes reported in the gospels can bear a positive interpretation. Jewish scholars studied not merely by private reading, but by setting up debates to test competing arguments. The Pharisees probably argued with each other, with no offence given or taken, almost as much as they argued with Jesus. Nevertheless, it remains true that the gospels represent the Pharisees, in general, as hostile to Jesus and his mission, and all four gospels record Jesus's own attacks on them. This long series of accusations in Matthew 23 is especially fierce.

The 'scribes' were the scholars, respected experts in the Jewish Law, who received the title 'Rabbi' – as Jesus sometimes does also. In turn, Jesus willingly compliments them (Matthew 13:52). Their education gave them an influential place among the religious leaders. Though they did not belong exclusively to any one party, they were principally associated with the Pharisees.

In the light of all this, we are not to imagine that Jesus rejects the scribes and Pharisees on principle. The words ascribed to him require his hearers to recognise their authority: 'do and observe what they tell you'. Even by the time the gospels were being written, maybe half a century after Jesus's death, there had been no final break between Judaism and Christianity. The immediate followers of Jesus never stopped thinking of themselves as faithful Jews, moulded and inspired by Jewish faith.

On the other hand, it is clear that the gospel condemnations do serve in part as a justification for a growing split between the respective *leaderships* of church and synagogue. It would be conceivable to read Matthew 23 as a straightforward description of the Jewish leadership, either that of Jesus's time or that of the period when the gospel was written, or to read it as a form of support for the leaders of the emerging Christian community, a disguised claim that they were morally superior to the scribes and Pharisees. But if these interpretations were adequate the passage would be at best a historical curiosity, and at worst a piece of propaganda, since the text unfairly blames the whole body of scribes and Pharisees for the sins of their worst representatives.

It is therefore important to realise that the gospels have a far more profound purpose than the kind of party political broadcast in which the whole object is to rubbish the opposition. They challenge, as well as encourage, *their own readers*. The words of the gospel remain relevant beyond the circumstances of their own day, because the evils identified can all too easily emerge in any religious group, and especially among its leaders. Therefore, we have to apply this text to our own lives and our own Church.

But before we can do that, another point needs to be considered. We mentioned the Pharisees' high and strenuous ideals. Ideals are pointless if they only reflect our present achievement. They serve to direct us forward, *beyond* our present failings and compromises. The term 'hypocrites', therefore, cannot simply refer to a group of people which fails to live up to its ideals, otherwise *every* preacher would stand accused of hypocrisy; still worse, the higher we aimed, the more hypocritical we would tend to become. Hypocrisy, rather, means the habit of systematically lying about one's ideals, in order that one's actual conduct escapes attention. The hypocrite's ideals are not truly *held*, they are only publicly proclaimed.

So we ought to be very slow to make the gospels' fiery language our own by accusing people of hypocrisy: after all, it is in Matthew, too, that we are told 'Do not judge, and you will not be judged' (7:1). But we are at least called to be alert to the constant danger that we will confuse our high religious ideals with our faltering practice. As an illustration of how readily this confusion can slip into the mentality of religious believers, we might consider the notion, fundamental to Roman Catholicism, of 'the Church'.

The term 'Church' may be given a 'common sense' meaning, by which it refers to a religious grouping which is visible to the world at large, is concretely present and active in society, is made up of institutions which have both excellences and faults, and whose members are a mixture of good and sinful people (or, more accurately, of people who are all in varying degrees *both* good and sinful). Alternatively, it may be used to denote that same group or system, *but only in so far as it is faithful to its vocation and inspiration.* Given the first meaning of the term, the Church embodies sin as well as grace. One might say, for example, 'For much of its history the Church has persecuted Jews'. Or again, the Church in this sense might *logically* be called 'corrupt' in some instance, even if the charge were, as a matter of fact, unfair. Given the second meaning of the word 'Church', though, such accusations would be nonsense; for as soon as people acted corruptly or oppressively they would have ceased to act as the Church!

In this book I have usually used the word 'Church' in the first sense. Official Church documents, on the other hand, more commonly speak of the Church in its second, 'high' sense. Either sense can be used with consistency and clarity. But there is a danger that the term will slide between one meaning and the other. Take, for example, the following extracts from a document issued by the Congregation for the Doctrine of the Faith in 1986, entitled *Christian Freedom and Liberation*:

> The evil inequities and oppression of every kind which afflict millions of men and women today openly contradict Christ's Gospel and cannot leave the conscience of any Christian indifferent.

The Church, in her docility to the Spirit, goes forth faithfully along the paths to authentic liberation. Her members are aware of their failings and their delays in this quest. (Section 57)

When the Church speaks out about the promotion of justice in human societies, or when she urges the faithful laity to work in this sphere according to their own vocation, she is not going beyond her mission . . . (Section 64)

She is likewise being faithful to her mission when she exercises her judgment regarding political movements which seek to fight poverty and oppression according to theories or methods of action which are contrary to the Gospel and opposed to man himself. (Section 65)

These passages rely on a sharp distinction between the Church itself and its members. That is, they treat the Church as a body which is *by definition* obedient to the Holy Spirit, faithful to the gospel and to 'authentic liberation'; whereas its members, naturally, have their failings. However, if we recognise this distinction, we must also notice what is implied in it, that the purity of 'the Church' is distinct from the truthfulness or wisdom of any of its members, including those who wrote this very document. However, the writers of *Christian Freedom and Liberation* seem instinctively to identify their own views about what is 'contrary to the Gospel' (which is occasionally a highly debateable subject) with the judgment of the Church itself. As it happens, they contradict certain opinions – about political movements, for instance – which are held by those who are also members of the Church. Such differences of practical judgment among Christians are inevitable and healthy. But the readers of *Christian Freedom and Liberation* are left uncertain whether the authors intend to contribute to a discussion and would welcome the expression of contrary views, or whether they mean to settle the matter in the name of the whole Church.

This ambiguity is not a matter of dishonesty, since the document probably relies on a broader concept which seeks to clarify the matter. According to the notion of the 'ordinary magisterium', official statements of the Church are to be presumed valid, even though they do not bind the Church itself. Nevertheless, it is doubtful that this remedy resolves the difficulty outlined here. To take seriously Jesus's accusation against the scribes and Pharisees is to recognise that those with religious authority (sinners, like the rest of us) can all too easily be led to exceed the limits of their proper function. In such a case they might claim to speak for the Church when they are really speaking for themselves. It follows, too, that watching out for such excessive claims is not a proof of 'disloyalty', or 'dissidence', but is one way of trying to be faithful to the gospel – always provided that we are equally alert to the modest status of *our own* claims!

It was argued in the second chapter, and it is presumed throughout this book, that the Church cannot fulfil its proper function unless it acts as a witness to and an agent of social justice. To take this stance does not commit us to the 'high' view that the Church fully embodies the qualities it stands for. For according to the 'common sense' view of the Church, social justice is not a *possession* of the church but is a *task* for it, a task which it has always to some extent assumed, but which it has carried out only fitfully. In fact, throughout its history, it has often practised injustice. If we take the alternative view, and *define* the Church as pure, we must admit that Church members, including Church leaders, have all too often been notably evil. They have been brutal, as when they have urged or carried out persecutions of the Jews and they have been personally vicious (as any history of the medieval papacy, for instance, will show vividly). Their formal claims to act as the Church were not less at such times. What is more, equivalent temptations face Church members and Church leaders in all ages, including our own – and few of them would deny it.

Let us return to the gospel and our story of Father Conroy. Matthew 23 reflects a situation in which the scribes and

Pharisees, the established religious authorities, are coming under an increasing challenge from the followers of Jesus, whose leaders hold a different understanding of what is fundamental to Jewish faith. A parallel conflict is illustrated by our story. The position of parish priest imposes on its holder an obligation that must not be neglected, for the parish's formation and growth in faith. Carrying out this task will force on him decisions he would prefer to avoid. Father Conroy is quite correct to see that Mrs Murphy's teaching and the project of the Justice and Peace Group pose a challenge to him. The 'Justice and Peace' movement within the Church, like the 'Christian Feminist' movement, makes a judgment about what is central to Christian faith and what is less central. It necessarily challenges other views about what is theoretically and practically fundamental. In particular, it implies that the more traditional sources of authority in the Church are legitimate, perhaps, but not absolute. Difficult questions immediately arise. Who decides what are the most important questions facing the Church today? How can the sources of authority be measured against each other, and who does the measuring? In our story, for instance, who decides how children in a Catholic school can best be helped to mature in their Christianity? Given sufficient trust in the good faith of others, the tension between these plural authorities will usually be manageable. But sometimes it will be expressed in open conflict; and certainly, it can never be resolved once and for all.

Our story is too brief to be able to give us a sense of Father Conroy's character and motivation. He might be acting out of the ingrained sense of many people in leadership positions that they know best and have the right to enforce their views on those who disagree (what Hamlet calls 'the insolence of office'). In that case, he would fall under the condemnation of Matthew 23, for he would be laying heavy burdens on people. He would not be 'allowing other people to go in who want to' (by using his own ignorant prejudice as the measure of permissible religious education); he would be 'having people call him Rabbi' (by insisting that he, and no one else, is the authentic teacher).

Alternatively, he might be acting out of a real fear that the schoolchildren will not be properly fed with the 'Good News', and that the proposed parish meeting will lead to more bitterness than enlightenment. In this second case, without some knowledge of Mrs Murphy and the Justice and Peace Group, we cannot estimate whether he is right or wrong, whether his fears are reasonable or stem from an unconscious refusal to consider arguments which make him feel insecure. The third, and quite likely, possibility is that both these motives co-exist!

But even if there are good reasons for Father Conroy's stance, there remains the question of *how* he exercises his leadership role in the parish. As it stands, the story suggests that he makes no effort to reach an understanding with the Justice and Peace Group. His explanation is abrupt and his position non-negotiable. In Matthew 20:25–7, Jesus says:

'You know that among the gentiles the rulers lord it over them, and great men make their authority felt. Among you this is not to happen. No; anyone who wants to become great among you must be your servant, and anyone who wants to be first among you must be your slave, just as the Son of man came not to be served but to serve, and to give his life as a ransom for many.'

Father Conroy 'pulls rank' on Mrs Murphy and the group: a servant or slave has no rank to pull.

This reflection leads to two separate conclusions. Firstly, Matthew 23 warns us that those who exercise leadership in the Church are not superior beings. They deserve respect, but they are not related to other Church members as parents to children ('Call no one on earth your father'), and we are not to defer to them automatically, without care or thought. By doing so, we would diminish them, by depriving them of the right to explore their own faith, to have mere, non-binding, opinions and uncertainties; and we would diminish ourselves by surrendering to them our consciences and initiative. But a second conclusion is no less important. Radical movements, including those in the Church, also have their temptations and pitfalls. A Justice and Peace Group or a feminist group could sometimes act out of antagonism to its opponents rather than out of a genuine 'hunger and thirst for uprightness' (Matthew 5:6). It might suffer from a rigid sense of its own righteousness, or rely on slogans which are as immune from questioning as the positions they oppose. In fact, those excluded from the presbytery by Father Conroy had better look to themselves, in case they begin to think like the Pharisee of Luke 18:9–14. We are all sinners: as a movement like Christian Feminism acquires a rightful authority within the Church, its leadership, also, will need to attend carefully to Matthew 23.

FOR REFLECTION

1. What do you understand by 'the Church'? Do you mean the whole Church, including yourself, or do you usually just mean the 'leadership' of the Church, or the 'institutional Church'? Might there be different leadership functions for different purposes?
2. If you ever have difficulties about the 'teachings of the Church' about doctrine or morals, how do you tend to react? Do you just disregard the teachings? Do you think again about your own position? Do you immediately assume you are wrong? Do you take advice – and if so, from whom?

PRAYER

Lord Jesus, may all those who follow you in your Church be faithful to the Gospel: may we become poor in Spirit and pure in heart. May we seek truth and justice with modesty and courage. Deliver us both from self-satisfaction and from cynicism, so that we may live in the hope that your promises can be fulfilled.

Prophetic Action

◆━━━◆

THROUGHOUT LENT, a Christian peace group had camped outside a nuclear base in Britain. They began on Ash Wednesday by calling for repentance in a nation that declared itself Christian, yet was willing to destroy whole populations. Every morning and evening they prayed together near the main gate.

Then, on Good Friday, four of them broke through the perimeter fence, sprayed the words 'All who draw the sword will die by the sword' on one of the office buildings, and gave themselves up to the guards. A few months later, they were brought to court on charges of criminal damage.

In their defence, the four admitted damaging the building, but denied that it could rightly be called '*criminal* damage'. They argued that their action was intended to avert destruction infinitely worse than any minor damage they had done; and that the likelihood of this destruction was increased as long as the Government felt able to assume the whole nation supported its 'defence' policy. Their act was designed to demonstrate that the nation was *not* unanimous. They pointed out that the slogan was taken from the warning spoken by Jesus in Matthew's gospel when one of his followers, in trying to defend him from arrest, cuts off the ear of the High Priest's servant. What was called in court a 'futile and threatening gesture', was therefore an attempt, made in good faith, to bring people to their moral senses. They were unarmed and posed no threat to the staff of the base.

The magistrate, however, insisted that only the action itself, the defacing of the building, and not the action's stated purpose, was relevant to the trial. He found them guilty, and sentenced them each to two weeks in prison.

◆━━━◆

(At the beginning of the reign of Zedekiah son of Josiah, king of Judah, this word came to Jeremiah from Yahweh:) Yahweh said this to me: 'Make yourself thongs and yokes and put them on your neck. Then send them to the king of Edom, the king of Moab, the king of the Ammonites, the king of Tyre, and the king of Sidon, through their envoys accredited to Zedekiah king of Judah in Jerusalem. Give them the following message for their masters, "Yahweh Sabaoth, God of Israel, says this: You must tell your masters this: I by my great power and outstretched arm made the earth, the human beings and the animals that are on earth, and I give them to whom I please. For the present, I have handed all these countries over to Nebuchadnezzar king of Babylon, my servant; I have even put the wild animals at his service. Any nation or kingdom that will not serve Nebuchadnezzar king of Babylon and will not bow its neck to the yoke of the king of Babylon, I shall punish that nation with sword, famine and plague, Yahweh declares, until I have destroyed it by his hand. For your own part, do not listen to your prophets, your divines, dreamers, magicians and sorcerers, who tell you: You will not be enslaved by the king of Babylon. They prophesy lies to you, the result of which will be that you will be banished from your soil, that I shall drive you out, and you will perish." ' . . .

The prophet Hananiah then snatched the yoke off the neck of the prophet Jeremiah and broke it. In front of all the people Hananiah then said, 'Yahweh says this, "This is how, in exactly two years' time, I shall break the yoke of Nebuchadnezzar king of Babylon and take it off the necks of all the nations." ' At this, the prophet Jeremiah went away.

*After the prophet Hananiah had broken the yoke he had
snatched off the prophet Jeremiah's neck, the word of
Yahweh came to Jeremiah, 'Go to Hananiah and tell him
this, "Yahweh says this: You have broken the wooden
yokes only to make iron yokes to replace them! For Yahweh
Sabaoth, the God of Israel, says this: An iron yoke is what
I now lay on the necks of all these nations, to enslave them
to Nebuchadnezzar king of Babylon." '*

(Jeremiah 27:1–6, 8–10; 28:10–14)

◆━━▶

Both Jeremiah and Hananiah are prophets who claim to
speak in the name of God. It is clear, though, that some
prophets are not what they pretend to be. In this passage,
the writer leaves us in no doubt whom we are to believe. We
are *shown* God speaking to Jeremiah, whereas Hananiah's
claims to receive a divine revelation are unsupported, and
presumably dishonest. According to the story, even God
takes Jeremiah's side, warning against 'your prophets, your
diviners, dreamers, magicians and sorcerers': God rejects
them by calling them 'yours' not 'mine'.

As we would expect, Jeremiah is proved right by events:
even before Chapter 28 is over, Hananiah, who has
'preached rebellion against Yahweh', is dead. But Jeremiah
can also be known to be a genuine prophet, the story suggests, because he preaches doom, not false comfort, and
because he is prepared to pay the price of unpopularity. In
Chapter 38, as a punishment for 'disheartening the remaining soldiers in the city' he is thrown into a well and left for
dead. (Similarly, a famous peace activist, Pat Arrowsmith,
was once jailed for undermining the morale of British
troops.) Yet, as the famous prophecy of Chapter 31 shows,
Jeremiah had a deeper vision and hope for the people than
they have for themselves.

It is striking that Jeremiah and Hananiah do not debate.
There is no calm or heated discussion about the future
political or military probabilities. Instead, they both employ
flamboyant, stagy gestures, which prove nothing of them-

selves but which undoubtedly grasp the attention of their audience. Sceptical onlookers might have shrugged and asked what on earth was the point, and presumed that their intelligence was being insulted. But both prophets' intention was to enact some sign to dramatise the state of affairs; and for Jeremiah, the authentic prophet, the truth of the situation is how it fits within the eternal and merciful plan of God.

This dramatic style of proclamation is quite common in the Bible. In Jeremiah 13, Jeremiah is instructed to perform such a sign by God's very self. He is to take his loincloth, or 'waistcloth', stuff it in a hole by the river Euphrates, and retrieve it years later, by which time, of course, it is 'ruined, no use for anything'. God explains that 'the pride of Judah, the immense pride of Jerusalem' will be ruined too: 'For just as a waistcloth clings to a man's waist, so I made the whole House of Israel and the whole House of Judah cling to me . . . But they have not listened'. In the gospels we see Jesus riding into Jerusalem on a donkey, washing his friends' feet in the middle of a meal, driving the market traders out of the Jerusalem Temple with a whip. All of these actions could unkindly be called unproductive or 'attention-seeking'. The Temple merchants, for sure, would be back next day!

Yet is is clear that Jesus is not the kind of impractical dreamer who gives no thought to the effectiveness with which the disciples carry out their mission. He does not suppose that faith and good intentions are a substitute for using one's brains. He tells his disciples, 'Look, I am sending you out like sheep among wolves; so be cunning as snakes and yet innocent as doves' (Matthew 10:16). Elsewhere he warns them not to make promises or undertake commitments rashly, without working out accurately whether they will be able to accomplish what they begin. They must have the shrewdness of a competent builder or army commander (Luke 14:28–33). The rueful conclusion he draws from the parable of the 'crafty steward' (Luke 16), is that 'the children of the world are more astute in dealing with their own kind than are the children of light'.

But our sense of what is practical and effective might sometimes be too narrow. It is always as well to be clear about the purpose of one's work: but this clarity ought not to mean that we restrict the range of worthwhile goals or appropriate styles of engagement to those cases where results are immediate or measurable. In particular, the pursuit of such a vast and elusive objective as 'social justice' is bound to require many different methods and skills. It will involve some people in the serious study of political theory or economics, others in local political organising. Some had better be present at the centre of a country's political power structure, for instance as MPs. They, especially, will need support, because their task is among the most difficult of all and they will be faced with the constant temptation to 'sell out', or to become bitter, or dishonest or manipulative. There will be important work to be done by teachers, in schools and in higher education. Others again will have to work patiently, probably without recognition, to build up a sense of dignity and community among those who are victimised or excluded by mainstream society. As a rule we shall need to be gentle, to appeal to the best in people, showing how their deepest purposes and values cannot be fulfilled without committing themselves to the search for justice. But sometimes we shall need the courage to condemn injustice, plainly and without fudging.

No one is versatile enough to accomplish all this, but neither ought anyone's talents to be written off as irrelevant. It is vital that the specialisms of some people do not discredit the different contribution which others can make. For example, those with trained intellectual ability can fulfil an indispensable function, by raising and analysing questions others are unwilling to think through, by investigating political or economic theories and their consequences. But politics is not only a matter of reason and compromise. It also involves passion, emotion, intuition. Sometimes what is needed is not intellectual argument, but a gesture to capture the public imagination, and transform the climate of the detailed debates – debates which will still need to go on. Yet anyone making such a 'prophetic' gesture will certainly be called 'naive' by their opponents, and will be accused of over-simplifying complex questions.

One famous modern example of such a gesture is that of the 'Salt March' organised by Mahatma Gandhi in 1930. As a leader in the Indian Congress, Gandhi had spent decades in the heat of practical politics. He had even spent years in prison. No one could have appreciated better than he how complex was the overall political situation. But in 1930 he focused on one single injustice. It was seemingly minor, but it summed up the entire oppressive system then experienced by native Indians. The Salt Act taxed a commodity which the very poorest people needed. It defined as criminal the manufacture or purchase of contraband salt. So Gandhi led a march of hundreds of miles to gather salt from the seashore. Throughout India, thousands who lived near the sea followed suit. The raw salt was boiled in pans and peddled. It must have seemed a crude tactic likely to backfire, especially when more than fifty thousand people were jailed in the aftermath of the march. Yet the Salt March may well have been a turning point in the whole history of the British Empire, because it succeeded in bringing to the surface, for all to see, the ruthlessness that underpinned imperial rule.

Perhaps there are few issues of today which are more intricate than that of peace and disarmament, especially nuclear disarmament. Even the sheer mechanical task of measuring one nation's stock of nuclear weapons against another's cannot be achieved without controversy, since weapons systems often cannot be directly compared: they have different ranges, different types of targets, some 'single' weapons have multiple warheads, and so on. At a deeper level, the pattern is dissolving by which the world has been dominated by the single confrontation of NATO and the Warsaw Pact. New and unstable patterns of alliances and enmities are emerging, and increasing numbers of nations are acquiring nuclear, biological or chemical weapons. What is more, much of the information we would need for a serious debate about decisions is unavailable, kept secret even from MPs: when leaks occur we can hardly be sure whether we are being better informed or deliberately misled. So, it could be argued, we can do nothing else but entrust responsibility to those in the know. Still more complexities emerge when other, related factors are taken into account. For military spending is so central to our Western economies that extensive disarmament will have profound and unpredictable economic consequences. Few people, probably, are competent to work out the implications.

All this makes it obvious that the search for peace will occupy the best intelligence of the world's diplomats and political scientists. In Britain, for instance, there is a specialist Department of Peace Studies at the University of Bradford. In such circumstances, it might appear simpleminded or juvenile to mount a protest of the kind outlined in our story. And yet we can hardly deny the need for anger and protest. Take our point about the level of military spending. It is clear that the scale of spending on armaments distorts virtually every national economy, siphoning off resources and skills that might otherwise alleviate international poverty. Pat Gaffney, General Secretary of Pax Christi, has drawn on the British Government's own defence estimates to show that 565,000 people are directly involved in the military industry, and that more than £2 billion of the £4.5 billion available from the government for research and development goes into military research.

The arms trade also corrupts every nation that engages in it. The leading military powers are virtually forced to recoup some of the immense cost of developing new weaponry by selling arms to other nations, no matter how oppressive their rulers or how desperate their economies. Two-thirds of Britain's arms sales goes to Third World countries: every year, Britain holds massive 'Arms Fairs' for this purpose. Such sales have immediate and fatal consequences. The poorer nations are left ever more dependent on their military suppliers, and, at the same time, less able to direct resources to their own neediest people. All too often, in fact, governments turn their expensive weapons on their own poorest people. And arms traders will be quite undeterred by the thought of supplying potential enemies, just as Britain and the USA supplied both Iran and Iraq in the 1970 and 1980s, and have supplied both Israel and the Arab nations over several decades. As Gaffney notes, thirteen major British companies attended Iraq's first International Exhibition for Military Production as recently as 1989.

Bruce Kent once told a useful parable about this trade. Imagine how the local police would respond if a stall was erected outside a big soccer ground on Saturday afternoon to sell knuckledusters and sheath knives. Imagine, too, how the Magistrates' Court would react to a plea from the seller that the knives were sold impartially to both sets of supporters. Yet that is the reality of the arms trade.

It is vitally important that *someone* should dramatise such mammoth irrationality, without being told they are naive for doing so. In fact, protest gestures do not imply that the issues at stake are simple, or attempt to do the experts' thinking for them. Instead, they seek to galvanise the wider community into thinking for itself about matters which are commonly, and disastrously, neglected. Their 'effectiveness' must be judged in the light of that objective.

None of us is in the privileged position of the writer of the book of Jeremiah, who is absolutely sure *which* prophet is on God's side and which one is opposed to God. We ourselves cannot help having to grope in the dusk of truth and for justice, and despite our best efforts, we might in every case be mistaken in our facts and judgments. The words of Jesus quoted by our protestors, 'All who draw the sword will die by the sword', are spoken to someone who presumably thought he was practising a justified and heroic act of resistance. (According to Matthew, the one who cut off the ear of the High Priest's servant was a 'follower' of Jesus; according to Mark, it was a 'bystander', and according to John it was Simon Peter himself!) What we can rightly expect of Christians who carry out such actions is that they scrutinise their own motives, that they themselves act non-violently (consistently with their professed aim), and that they act in a spirit of prayer. Equally Christians concerned for peace have an obligation to respond to such actions by rethinking their own position, and to avoid concluding carelessly or impatiently that all such demonstrations are the work of fanatics. There are some evils, as Jesus insists, that 'can be driven out only by prayer' (Mark 9:29): but, as always, this prayer must inspire our action not be a substitute for it.

FOR REFLECTION

1. What do you think are the main characteristics of a 'true prophet'? Can we identify genuine prophets only with hindsight, or it is possible to recognise certain prophets in our own day?
2. Would you say that the overall media coverage of recent international wars (the Gulf War, perhaps, or the Falklands War of 1982) conveyed a sufficiently accurate impression of war; of its terror, of the suffering of its victims, of its consequences? Is there a difference between reasonable national morale-boosting and mere 'propaganda'?
3. An American humorist defined peace as 'a period of cheating between two periods of fighting'. Do you find yourself thinking that the 'peace movement' is unrealistic, or childish, or unbalanced? What would 'balance' mean in this matter?

PRAYER

Lord Jesus, who said to your disciples, 'A peace which the world cannot give, this is my gift to you', fill us with the desire for that peace which is the fruit of justice between nations, and send your Spirit to enlighten us as to how to work towards it.

The Transforming Spirit

MARGARET WAS A SHY, even timid woman in her fort-
ies, married with two children. She liked her job as a junior
school teacher, but had few interests outside school. Now
that her children were growing up, she sometimes hardly
knew what to do with her time. She had once gone through
a phase where she watched TV for two or three hours every
evening to keep her husband company, until she discovered
that she never got up from the chair without the dissatisfied
feeling, that it had been 'a waste of time'. Then she decor-
ated the kitchen twice in one year, deciding she didn't much
like the first colour scheme. Sometimes she had the feeling
that her real life was over, and that all she had to look
forward to was a kind of second career as a baby-sitter and
granny.

One day, two children in her class were beaten up on
their way home from school. They lived with their family
on a site set aside by the Council for travelling people, and
for some time they had been subjected by a few classmates
to teasing, then to insults. Margaret had noticed the situation developing, but apart from warning the other children
to stop bullying, had done nothing.

Now she decided to go round to the site to speak to the
injured children's parents. She'd had to pluck up the courage
to do this, expecting to be personally blamed for the incident. To her surprise she was warmly welcomed, and taken
to meet another teacher, who ran a small schoolroom in a
portakabin on the site. Almost before she knew what was

happening Margaret had been co-opted onto a 'Support Group' for the travellers. Within a few months the group organised a playscheme, negotiated with the local authority about conditions on the site and protested to two doctors who had refused to treat the travellers because they turned up dirty. Margaret even went to a local tenants' meeting and opposed the almost unanimous opinion of her neighbours that the Council should be pressed to expel the travellers from the site because they were a 'nuisance'.

To her surprise, Margaret found she was well-suited to this kind of work. She had never thought of herself as a 'political' person, still less as an activist. She still preferred taking a back seat within the support group: but she was becoming quite expert in social welfare and legal provisions as they affected travellers, and she found herself in increasing demand as an advisor, not only to the travellers but to many other people.

◆━━━◆

[Jesus said to the disciples]

> *They will expel you*
>   *from the synagogues,*
> *and indeed the time is coming*
> *when anyone who kills you*
>   *will think he is doing*
>   *a holy service to God.*
> *They will do these things*
> *because they have never known*
>   *either the Father or me.*
> *But I have told you all this,*
> *so that when the time for it comes*
> *you may remember that I told you . . .*
>
> *Still, I am telling you the truth:*
> *it is for your own good that I am going,*
> *because unless I go,*
> *the Paraclete will not come to you;*

but if I go,
I will send him to you . . .

I still have many things to say to you
but they would be too much for you
   to bear now.
However, when the Spirit of truth comes
he will lead you to the complete truth,
since he will not be speaking
   of his own accord,
but will say only what he has been told;
and he will reveal to you
   the things to come.
                              (John 16:2–4, 7, 12–13)

Margaret's life, it appears, has been suddenly and unexpectedly transformed by the kind of unfortunate event that occurs every day but leaves most people unaffected. She has 'realised' gifts of which she was not previously aware: that is, she had discovered them, and she has put them to use. Her customary timidity no longer obscures a genuine courage. She is 'free' in a way she perhaps was not before, is no longer enslaved to the prejudices of people she still lives among: and this positive new force in her is not driven by private, self-centred goals, but has been evoked by the need of others. Christians would see this revolution in her consciousness as the work of the Holy Spirit.

The gift of the Spirit, in one of its aspects, can be seen as a fulfilment of the word of God spoken through the prophet Joel:

> 'I shall pour out my spirit on all humanity.
> Your sons and daughters shall prophesy,
> your old people shall dream dreams,
> and your young people see visions.
> Even on the slaves, men and women,
> shall I pour out my spirit in those days.'
>   (Joel 3:1–2)

The Spirit, then, can enable us to perceive the world more fully, even more joyfully. This gift of *vision* is perhaps conveyed to us especially through the work of artists. It is strikingly expressed by the poet and painter William Blake:

> I know that this world is a world of imagination and vision. I see everything I paint in this world, but everybody does not see alike. To the eye of a miser a guinea is far more beautiful than the sun . . . The tree which moves some to tears of joy is in the eyes of others only a green thing which stands in the way.

But visionary ecstasy is not enough for a life in the Spirit. The true gift of the Holy Spirit also fulfils the very practical promise of Jesus. His 'going to the Father', he says, will permit the gift of the 'Paraclete', so 'It is for your own good that I am going'. This 'Paraclete' will be for the disciples everything that Jesus has been for them while he was alive and in their midst. It remains 'his' Spirit. But its power is not to be confined by the limits of space and time. It is an old Christian adage, for instance, that the action of the Spirit is not confined to the sacraments or to the visible Church, but is like the wind which 'blows where it pleases' (John 3:7–8). In the power of the Spirit, Jesus insists, the disciples 'will perform the same works as I do myself, and will perform even greater works' (John 14:12).

The word 'Paraclete' contains several shades of meaning: it signifies at once helper, consoler and strengthener, advocate. All these meanings might reasonably have troubled the disciples. If they need a consoler or strengthener, they are clearly going to suffer. If they need a helper or advocate, perhaps they will be overwhelmed with work or in trouble with the authorities: indeed, John's gospel links the promise of the Spirit with the promise of persecution.

Even the varied meanings of the term 'Paraclete' do not exhaust the New Testament images of the Holy Spirit. In our extract, Jesus refers to the 'Spirit of truth' who will lead the disciples towards 'complete truth'. The 'Pentecost' text, in the Acts of the Apostles, speaks of wind and fire; elements which, when combined, cause a fierce blaze! St Paul often speaks of the Spirit which brings freedom (e.g. Romans 8:2, 22–5; 2 Corinthians 3:17).

It seems, then, that we can identify the presence of the Holy Spirit whenever we become convinced that qualities which are normally difficult to combine co-exist: passionate courage, inner freedom, a love of truth even where the truth might be disadvantageous. It is only this 'integrity' which can fulfil our deepest human longings: or, to put the same thing another way, we can have no final fulfilment except in and through the Holy Spirit.

Of course, the 'freedom' we sometimes find ourselves desiring might have little connection with truth or courage: we speak casually of 'freedom of choice' or 'freedom from worry'. Every good quality can, in a certain sense, exist apart from the Spirit: but then it becomes less fully human too. So, order can become regimentation; community can be reduced to alliances; recreation to 'time off'; patience to apathy. The Scriptures, for example, speak of 'reconciliation' as a ministry of Christ which is given to his followers to carry forward (2 Corinthians 5:18–19). But there is even a degenerate version of 'reconciliation'. In Luke's account of the Passion of Jesus, in Chapter 23, Pontius Pilate sends Jesus to Herod for trial, so tactfully recognising Herod's right to judge such cases. But when Herod gets no satisfaction from Jesus, he sends him back to Pilate, to his doom. Luke comments grimly, 'though Herod and Pilate had been enemies before, they were reconciled that day'. In our own day, Saul Alinski has written of the squalid transaction by which 'the rich keep the money and the poor get reconciled to it'. Evidently, not all reconciliation is of the Spirit.

In our story, though, Margaret grows in truth, freedom and courage. She comes to reject a false assessment of her duties and her limitations. She is a teacher, a housewife, a local resident. As a teacher she could get away with ignoring what goes on outside the school gates. Now she is prepared to be personally implicated, to do something to protect those who are being ill-treated. As a housewife, she had perhaps felt obliged to keep her husband company, even if the TV programmes bored her stiff. She now realises that his choice to watch TV does not compel her to make the same choice, for she is her husband's wife, not her husband's *person*. As a local resident, she might well have assumed she had better stick up for her neighbours, even when they appeared at their most mean-minded. Now she is prepared to confront them. She has realised, in fact, that each of the roles she lives out can either express or betray her true being. She cannot escape from playing such roles, but she is aware that they can diminish her.

This is a universal problem, and is therefore a universal task and point of growth. Doctors, for instance, experience considerable pressure to conform to others' stereotypes: they can therefore hide their doubts, their occasional ignorance, the possibility that they will make mistakes, their own need to be supported and reassured. The job of a bartender brings with it the almost overpowering presumption that one will be good-humoured, tolerant, non-judgmental and keep one's own beliefs well under wraps. Imagine the bar steward, man or woman, who dared to object angrily to a customer's dirty joke or flirtatious sexual proposition or anti-semitic remark. Again, if you are unemployed in Britain a definite role is expected of you. The nation might pay your benefit as long as you have the tact to look miserable – but you had better not be seen to enjoy yourself! A priest will immediately cause offence if he is seen to be too obviously close to a woman – or a man. In each instance, a natural courtesy, a disposition to behave the way others expect us to, can impede our own honesty or spontaneity, can block the growth of strong and tested convictions.

The fuller, more engrossing, more satisfying is the role, the more difficult is freedom with respect to it. An assembly-line worker is hardly likely to think her role as employee ought to express her whole personality. She may even find that she only 'comes alive' on leaving the factory gate. A job for her will probably be little more than an unfortunate necessity, a way of paying for her 'real life'. It is, of course, a serious social evil when people can expect no more than that from their employment. On the other hand, a social worker, for example, drawn to that vocation by a particular enthusiasm and set of ideals, may be able to express far more of her real self through her paid job: but if she fails to realise that her personhood goes beyond her identity as a social worker, both her work and her life outside work will suffer. At work she will be tense, prone to 'burn-out': elsewhere she might begin to assume a misplaced and intrusive responsibility for the lifestyle and decisions of her friends and family.

Roles can be corporate, also. Party politics can impose on politicians a tiresome ritual of automatic disagreement. The opposition parties can feel bound to reject whatever ministers propose, and end up taking government policy more seriously than the government itself does. Even the practice of morality and the commitment of social justice can shrink to the acting out of a hackneyed role. The moralist can be all too sure of what is right and wrong, addicted to the harsh judgment of others. Those who commit themselves to work for justice can come to inhabit a world of predigested and constantly repeated slogans, their critical intelligence crippled by their acceptance of a few crude category-words ('bourgeois'; 'Thatcherite') as accurate descriptions of social reality. Even the important corrective insights can turn sour. The ecology movement has demonstrated that social justice cannot consist of a mere extension of Western consumerism across the globe. Equally, though, that movement could itself be perverted, and itself come to deny the Spirit, if it became the intellectual defence mechanism of those affluent societies who were determined above all to reserve their wealth to themselves. And there is indeed a version of 'concern for the environment' which smacks of just this: among those people, for example, who are eager to impose population control on the Third World as a substitute for supporting the development of its economies.

All social movements and ideals have their perversion.

The authentic and the corrupted expressions cohabit at the heart of each, and cannot easily be distinguished. What Christians understand by Spirit is that Power, that Gift, which both purifies and strengthens each of us individually, and our communities together. An authentic, Spirit-filled, search for justice will at the same time lead us towards our own fuller humanity, by way of a growing love for freedom and for truth-telling. And the Spirit frees us not from the giving of self in service to others, but from being enslaved by that service. As St Paul writes to the Christian community in Rome,

Do not model your behaviour on the contemporary world, but let the renewing of your minds transform you, so that you may discern for yourselves what is the will of God – what is good and acceptable and mature.

(Romans 12:2)

FOR REFLECTION

1. The Christian Scriptures often contrast 'Spirit' and 'flesh'. What is the point of this contrast?
2. Why should we expect the Spirit to *unite* the Christian community? Is it not more likely that many people's reception of diverse gifts will lead to more difficult tensions?
3. Everyone, presumably, lives out a variety of different roles. Is the ideal of 'integration' therefore only a fantasy? What could it mean in practice?
4. If we strive always to be 'open to everyone', will it ever be possible to fight for urgent causes?

PRAYER

Lord God, you will make all things new and will renew the face of the earth. Send out your Spirit so that we your people might also be created anew. Strengthen and enlighten us, who pray to be faithful followers of Jesus your Son.

Postscript

SOME OF THE EXAMPLES of justice and injustice we have considered can be tackled primarily on the individual level. But other cases are 'structural', concerned with the character of certain groups, systems or institutions, and the relationships between them. Where such a public situation is evil, no individual can be 'blamed' for it. Equally, any effective response is beyond the power of a single unaided person. Therefore, it may be appropriate to draw attention to a very few of the Church-based bodies which are involved with issues of justice in Britain and overseas. All of them would welcome your interest. All of them are charities, and cannot sustain their work without financial support.

Catholic Fund for Overseas Development (CAFOD),
2 Romero Close, Stockwell Road, London SW9 9TY

Church Action on Poverty (CAP),
Central Buildings, Oldham Street, Manchester M1 1JT

Catholic Institute for International Relations (CIIR),
22 Coleman Fields, London N1 7AF

Pax Christi,
St Francis of Assisi Centre, Pottery Lane, London W11 4NQ

Scottish Catholic International Aid Fund (SCIAF),
43 Greenhill Road, Rutherglen Glasgow G73 2SW